Achtung! Sw...

Merchant Aircraft Carriers

by

Stanley Brand

Winged Escort

by Terry Lee

This book is published by Propagator Press, an imprint of:

AMS Educational
Woodside Trading Estate
Low Lane
Horsforth
Leeds LS18 5NY

ISBN   1 86029 805 2

Designed by Propagator Press
Printed in Great Britain

Stanley T. Brand
Sub Lieut. (A) R.N.V.R Aged 22
At the end of the war in Europe

Whilst every effort has been made to trace the copyright holders of the photographs used in this book, this has not always been possible. Stanley Brand would like to thank all those people whose pictures have contributed to his story.

Dedication

Dedicated To The Sisters

Fairey Swordfish and Blackburn Swordfish

and to their designers, builders, aircrew, ground crew, Royal and Merchant Navy ships and men who bore them over the seas, and above all, to those who had their precious lives taken from them in the service of their country whilst performing the many deeds of gallantry carried out by the crews of Swordfish.

Especially to my own aircrew, Observer Sub Lieutenant William Thomson RNVR and Telegraphist Air Gunner, Petty Officer John Hopkins neither of whom lived to enjoy the fruits of the peace they helped to win, and who never received the recognition they so richly deserved for their valiant efforts.

Also to the surviving Swordfish, to those who saved them from premature destruction, to those who resurrected them, to those who nurse and finance them in their old age, and particularly to the young men who are interested, keen and capable enough to take over from the present team of custodians and keep Swordfish flying for many years into the future.

May God bless them and all who give their support.

Stanley Brand

Stanley Brand

Stanley T. Brand
In 1998, aged 75, after flying in W5856 again

Acknowledgements

The author acknowledges, with grateful thanks, the advice, encouragement and assistance given to him by Catherine Brand, Bob Buck, Graham Winship, Carolyn Ryder, Alan J. Mitchell, Berna Councell, Jonathan Pink, Lt.Cdr.Bruce Vibert D.S.C., C.D., R.C.N.R., Lt. Cdr. Roy Portchmouth, R.C.N.R., June Smith, Ted Powell, Richard Crapp, Cdr John Beattie RN, Mike Parsons and many others, without whose help a word processor would have been hurled into a rubbish dump, his ignorance of spelling and grammar would have been exposed to all, and his confused concept of middle, finis and beginning would have bewildered even those few loyal friends persistent enough to read through to the end. I hope, my friends, it was worth all the trouble you took and that reading it to the finish was not prompted by the fact that you had to buy your copy. (All proceeds go to the Swordfish Heritage Trust, which maintains Swordfish W5856 in an airworthy condition. I flew, and pranged, this aircraft in 1944 and feel some responsibility towards the prolongation of its active life.)

At the age of 81, the implausibility of some of the details I remember is matched only by the clarity with which they are recalled, but my flying log-book provided the main source of hard fact. Filtering out the discrepancies has been no mean task, and I plead for your forgiveness for residual errors and I offer the excuse that frailty of mind pursues me with growing efficiency and at a great rate of knots.

As one who trained in sciences, and is devoid of any active artistic ability, I am overwhelmed by the competence of Terry Lee, the painter of "Winged Escorts" to depict the atmosphere as if he had trundled around convoys for most of his life. It is indeed a privilege to be given his permission to use his magnificent work to illustrate my book. I am deeply indebted to him.

Stanley Brand

Merchant Aircraft Carrier, Motor Vessel *Alexia*

Unusual view on take-off. The air gunner was usually looking back and upwards at the deck, which was rarely horizontal. The warmth and stillness of a summer's evening shows a degree of tranquillity, which is foreign to the general fury of the North Atlantic.

Contents

Foreword

The heading I have given to Chapter Two is a deliberate misquotation from *The Pilgrim's Progress*. It should read 'The Slough of Despond' instead of 'The Trough of Despond' but the latter befits the circumstances of the Battle of the Atlantic much more appropriately. In a slough the mire is so overwhelming, so imprisoning, that the more one struggles the greater the entrapment and the worse one's predicament becomes until exhaustion deprives the victim of the will to continue the struggle. In a trough one can assess the steepness of the side just descended and therefore know the magnitude of the task of extricating oneself. Facing up to reality and planning to overcome the problem is the sure way to success. In our Battle <u>with</u> the Atlantic we knew that we could never be the victor, but with our human opponents it was a different matter. We saw our way out of the trough of despondency and fought to get there.

This is our story . . .

Stanley Brand, Q Flight
836 Naval Air Squadron
Macship Wing
Fleet Air Arm

Chapter One

The Straggler

It would have been very easy to miss her, but Johnny spotted her through the gloom and spindrift, about a mile away, her stern low in the water, listing steeply to port and with no sign of motion through the water. Worse still, there was not the slightest wisp of smoke from her tall, old-fashioned funnel as she lay beam-on to the run of the waves. We flew as low as possible, and circled her to see what we could. We were met with frantically waving shirts and towels from a cluster of about ten people, all crammed into the wheel-house and open bridge, areas which had taken a terrible battering from the storm of last week.

Johnny Hopkins, our Telegraphist Air Gunner was, with his Aldis lamp, already flashing his Morse-code letters very slowly to speak to mariners who had a foreign language and were probably unpractised in this form of communication. His message went something like this- "Name ship please. What problems have you?" While waiting for their reply, which was very slow in coming, Bill Thomson, (our Observer) and I were assessing the obvious damage to this poor old tramp steamer of about eighteen hundred tons and of first-world-war vintage. She had probably been laid-up and suffered neglect during the world-wide slump of the 1930s and had been brought out of unemployment straight into the demands of wartime convoys. Her hatch covers were in disarray, showing broken timbers and torn tarpaulins which would give access to her holds for the wild and angry seas of the hurricane weather we had experienced, and would explain her severe list and being down at the stern. Her mast had broken off a few feet above the deck, probably due to her wallowing beam-on to wave crest and trough, carrying with it the wireless aerial and the derricks used for cargo handling. The resulting entanglement lay over the port waist of the ship and contributed to the severe list. Empty davits and lifeboat debris sculling around showed where the ship's boats had been smashed by the thunderous waves.

The answer to our questioning established the identity of the ship as the last of the six merchant ships which we had been sent to round-up and direct back to our convoy, following their uncontrollable scattering by the overwhelming storm which hit us, a not unusual experience in the North Atlantic in winter. We had flown, in our three-seat, single-engine Fairey "Swordfish" open-cockpit biplane (the only aircraft capable of performing the task demanded) from our Merchant Navy Aircraft Carrier (Macship). This was an oil-tanker, of 8,000 tons, carrying its normal cargo, manned by a civilian Captain and crew, supplemented by Fleet Air Arm personnel to operate three Swordfish from a miniature flight-deck without a hangar.

The rest of the almost unintelligible reply conveyed to us the nightmare predicament in which the unfortunate crew were placed. Memory after nearly sixty years cannot be precise, but I recall the pathos conveyed by the simplicity of their wording. "Engine broke. No steer. Fires out. Engine room flooded. Pumps broke. Mate leg broke. Stokerman arm and ribs broke. No lifeboat. Wireless gone. SOS please".

Bill, whose two weeks of seniority over me put him in command, wasted no time in discussion and told Johnny to reply "We fetch help soon", and he gave me a guesstimated heading to go back on our tracks to the nearest merchantman which we had located and to whom we had given a bearing to rejoin the convoy. I immediately turned on to this approximation while Bill concentrated on plotting an exact course to intercept that ship, which did not know it was going to be the salvation of a ship's crew in distress. Within minutes, Bill gave me the correction, which I applied, keeping my eyes skinned for the potential rescuer. I was worried because to get back to our Macship (Merchant Aircraft Carrier) we would be flying into a headwind which seemed to me to be increasing rapidly in force, but kept my doubts to myself as I could not distract Bill from his concentrated and complicated navigation upon which our lives and those of others depended. I had a tank of fuel run down to a barely safe level after a long and widespread hunt, in poor visibility, to round up stragglers over an area of forty by forty miles and now we were undertaking a commitment, which would probably demand more fuel than we had left. Our parody of the RAF motto "Per *ardua ad astra"* seemed likely to become a sick joke. It was *"Per ardua ad aqua"*, altering "Through hardships to the stars" to a bowdlerised "Through hardships, *We* end up in the drink."

One of the major drawbacks of flying from Macships, was the inadequate length of the flight deck, and the absence of variable pitch propellers, which were not available to us, because – we were told – the RAF had contracts with all the production capacity for variable pitch gear. So our fixed pitch propeller had to be of permanently fine pitch, essential to get enough power to lift our heavy loads from a tiny flight deck. This imposed a limit on the cruising character of the Swordfish, comparable to driving a car in permanent low gear on a motorway, giving extra power on take-off, but over-revving except at painfully low speed, causing undesirable wear and the drinking of fuel at an alarming rate.

With a full load, consisting of eight rockets with armour-picrcing warheads (when the cloud base allowed an attacking height from 1000 feet), or four x 500lb. depth charges (when patrolling at a lower height, as we were today), the cruising speed was seventy two knots at 2150 r.p.m., about eighty m.p.h.. If the gale developed to a forty-five knot blow coming from the direction of the convoy as a headwind to us, the ground speed of the aircraft would be 72-45=27 knots and the closing speed on a seven-knot convoy would be 27-7=20 knots. Operating forty sea miles behind a convoy would demand two hours of flying just to catch up. Perhaps our wisest course of action would be to ditch beside a seaworthy ship, which might be able to pick us up?

Having always been aware that the "Sheepdog Trials", rounding up strays, created a serious danger under these circumstances, I always paid attention to the fuel indicator gauge before switching off after a flight, and compared it with the tank capacity minus the fuel required to fill up as reported on the form 700 log kept meticulously by my ground crew. Having become suspicious of the accuracy of the gauge, I had foolishly had it replaced after my last flight, without stopping to think that I had replaced what check I had established with a completely unknown quantity in a new instrument.

It must be difficult for anyone who flew solely from airfields to understand our predicament. Why didn't we radio for help? It was because we were committed to radio and radar silence unless we were in close and immediate contact with the enemy when, our position would be known to him anyway. Both radio and radar transmissions could be picked up by a device known as Metox, a French invention used by the Germans, to home aircraft or submarines on to the transmitter. Breaking silence unnecessarily was a court martial offence, with a charge of endangering the safety of the convoy. Acts of self-preservation were looked down upon, as un-heroic, as will be illustrated in two incidents described in later chapters. We could not afford to risk the safety of our tanker, the one and only place to land within a radius of 1000 miles. A land-based aircraft could always divert to another airfield, and had extensive and sound meteorological information to forewarn the crew of the need to do so, benefits not available to us. If ever a choice arose between endangering the safety of a convoy or its escort, against deliberately sacrificing a comparatively small number of lives then the sacrifice had to be made.

Of course Bill understood the implication of my statement that we had about two hours' duration left at most economical cruising speed, coming as it did when we turned away from the convoy to retrace our course. Hightailing along with the strong wind at our backside, we were soon approaching the spot where Bill had calculated that we would find the ship we were looking for, and sure enough I spotted her by the clouds of thick, black, greasy smoke that poured out of her downwind in a straight line away from the convoy.

She was digging into the roller crests at the greatest speed that her stokers and engineers could squeeze out of her coal-fired boilers and reciprocating steam engine. Her captain was keen to get back to the safety of the convoy, and would not be very happy at the onerous task we were about to impose on him. Safety did I say? I will frequently repeat that safety in the North Atlantic in the middle of a ruthless war was purely comparative and nowhere could be considered safe. Tomorrow could bring a reversal of roles and that captain could be in need of a life-saving hand himself, so his full cooperation was assured.

Bill had already passed to Johnny a note of the signal to be flashed to the ship, giving the bearing and distance to the victim of the storm, stressing the urgency of the necessary action. We, in the Swordfish, who were impotent to provide physical assistance, were delighted to see the kick of white water at the rudder, which signified the change of course of the Samaritan, to effect a rescue. There was no more for us to contribute except to try to get back to our carrier, refuel and make ourselves ready to fly again, so we wasted no time at all in heading for our Macship at the speed reckoned to give maximum coverage of distance for the minimum consumption of petrol. Intuition can be remarkably accurate when your life depends upon it!

As I felt an icy chill sweep over me, I realised how much I had been sweating over the last few hours, in spite of the icy conditions within my cockpit, open to the whirlwind blast of the slipstream in below-zero temperatures. In those days we had not heard of wind-chill factors but we knew what they were because we could feel them. Safety harness, tightened up hard against the unpredictable bumps and surges of gusting and erratic wind, restricted even the slightest movement and thus interfered with circulation. These facts, together with an awareness of our own predicament made me clench my teeth to stop them chattering.

Bill commented calmly that the white horses on wave crests had increased enormously due to an increase in headwind, which he estimated to be of the order of ten knots, but that we wouldn't waste petrol by manoeuvring to determine exact wind speed and direction. I suddenly felt an overwhelming urge to pass the urine, which I had been holding for the past three hours. No Swordfish I ever flew had official provision for this essential but I had improvised a primitive facility. It was a paraffin funnel, (the smallest one available) inserted into a length of garden hose, which exited on the lee side of the fuselage. Here it was sheltered from the spiralling blast of the slipstream, which could cause blow-back problems. The improvisation was less than satisfactory because of the difficulty of lining-up the many differing access flies in the multiple layers of clothing obligatory in Arctic conditions, giving a much-extended route, which was made impossible by the inadequacy of the member concerned at prevailing temperatures. It was a case of sending Mohammed to the mountain instead of the converse, and the mouth of the funnel needed to pass through the flies, without success. The temporary warmth was no consolation for the chill which followed, nor for the problems of laundering my oiled-wool long-johns, (known as "Scapa-scanties").

In the euphoria which followed relief of this pressing need it would have been very easy to close my eyes and relax into a comatose state if it had not been for our almost frantic need to spot the convoy before our faithful Pegasus engine ground to a halt from the lack of fuel, a stimulus which was very effective.

The rear of the convoy was at least seven miles wide with columns a thousand yards apart so we knew that even in the poor visibility it would be impossible to miss, provided we could reach it before running out of petrol. We began to see all the careless telltale signs of a convoy which could lead a U-boat to its victims: the contents of a "gash bin", (i.e. a trash bin), floating on the surface, dumped so recently that they had not become waterlogged and dispersed, or a cigarette packet made of flimsy wartime cardboard but not yet disintegrated. Oil slicks were another giveaway, as recent ones hung together, whereas older ones were dispersed by waves in a few days depending on the viscosity of the oil.

At last I picked out something different in the welter of broken water at a distance of about one and a half miles on our port bow. There was no joy or relief in this until we could be sure what the object was. It was quite a common occurrence for a U-boat to be surprised on the surface behind a convoy, with the attention of their excited lookouts being temporarily distracted from astern by their sighting of potential victims ahead. Handicapped by an empty main fuel tank, and running for the last five minutes on "emergency reserve" was not the best time to be blessed with a long-awaited sighting of an unsuspecting sea-wolf. The thought of our engine spluttering and coughing to a halt, forcing us to an ignominious ditching in the middle of an attack, followed by being picked out of the water by the U-boat and taken back to Lorient as prisoners of war, didn't appeal to us. At last, through his Admiralty binoculars, Bill recognised the grey shape, awash in heavy seas, as a Flower class corvette and we were able to give our whole attention to looking out for our flight deck again. The presence of an escorting rearguard gave us confidence. We had a good chance of being picked up if we ditched before reaching our Macship operating in the open "box" cleared of other shipping in the centre of the convoy. With a little bit of searching we spotted her at last, ideally situated and travelling dead into wind. Bill flashed the carrier with our identity and predicament as follows - "Q3 out of fuel coming straight in".

Without any wasted time, that is just what happened. Once we were safely aboard, our sighs of relief, were equalled by those issuing from the bridge. We hadn't realised how popular we were, but we might have guessed from the first class state of readiness with which they received us, as they had been standing by to take us on board, worrying for us for the last forty minutes.

We hurried up to the bridge to report the situation of the vessel in distress and our Air Staff Officer (ASO) sent a signal to the Senior Officer of the Escort (SOE), with a repeat to the Commodore of the Convoy (CoC). Shortly we received the reply "Unable to spare an escort to add to action taken already by your aircrew which is best available under circumstances. Monitor situation by air."

This was followed by an endorsement from the CoC. Our reaction and that of our ship's company was one of great disappointment, and my own ground crew became almost mutinous when they refuelled my Swordfish and their meter read 165 gallons. The Swordfish specification reads: - Fuel Capacity Main 155 gallons, Emergency Reserve 12 and one-half gallons.

Said at a volume I was intended to hear, was the comment "Why would any sane person risk his neck when the top brass won't lift a finger to help when things go wrong". I had to take the commentator on one side and tell him that whilst my first feelings were in agreement with his, they explained why neither he nor I would ever be given the overwhelming responsibility of commanding an escort, and we must be thankful for the bravery and guts of men capable of giving such unbearable decisions for the common good. I also commented that I was never included in the category "a sane person" Word got round, the grumbles disappeared and banter was restored.

My ground crew were a wonderful crowd who worked in appalling conditions on an exposed flight deck in stormy Arctic temperatures, handling freezing metal by the light of a torch with failing batteries, to get my aircraft serviced ready to fly again as quickly as possible. On this occasion there was nothing to be gained by returning to the stricken vessel in the dark, but it was programmed that I would take-off to be there at first light in the morning. The ground crew worked on whilst I got some essential sleep, and the instrument fitter left notes under my door, in the briefing room and taped to my joystick, all saying the same thing, that my fuel gauge was reading about ten gallons less than there really was were a real lifesaver.

Next morning the ground team started work about 90 minutes before scheduled take-off, and had MQ3 (M signifying 836 squadron of the Macship Wing, Q for Q flight and 3 for the junior aircraft and aircrew in a flight of three) ready to be manned for take-off. The wind had dropped considerably, down to about 20 knots and the salt spray was no longer reaching the flight deck. The pitching and roll on the flight deck had reduced from 25 feet and 15 degrees to around 15 feet and 15 degrees respectively, but still enough to tie my stomach in knots. At the briefing I was advised that in the last ten hours the convoy had made 53 sea miles westerly of the position where I landed-on last night. We were about 80 miles from our straggler's grave if opening her sea-cocks had been effective. My flight to check on this was cancelled because of an Asdic report from the corvette escort on the starboard wing of the convoy, demanding immediate investigation. Progress of the survivors heading back to the convoy was of lesser importance. That is another story saved for later.

I must try to explain the general situation, and why we were doing what we did in the North Atlantic and the methods of selection and training we were given to enable us to carry out the tasks we performed. This book is an attempt to let following generations know of the dedication and fellowship of their forebears engaged in the struggle to survive the U-boat menace in the North Atlantic during the Second World War.

The Crew of Queenie Three
Left to right: Stan Brand, Johnny Hopkins and Bill Thomson

Chapter Two

The Trough of Despond

It is February 1942. Short days, black nights and black news. America had her Navy decimated at Pearl Harbour three months ago in the sneak attack by the Japanese and the Far East is falling rapidly to Japanese land forces. Rommel is rampaging through North Africa and U-boat wolf packs are dominating the Atlantic. Almost the whole of the European continental coastline is in the hands of German forces. Britain is in a desperate situation.

Our lifeline of food, oil and military supplies from the vast storehouse and production potential of the American continent, is in danger of being severed and without it we will perish. Already our civilians are rationed to the limit in food, clothing and fuel to such a degree that any further cuts must damage the wonderful spirit of defiance that has been shown towards the Nazi aggressor. To survive the German inroads to her heartland, Russia is demanding the opening of a "Second Front" by the Allies in the West, to draw German men and materials from the Russian Front. Such action is a long way off and it may never happen if we cannot keep the sea lanes open, allowing us to accumulate a surplus, after we have met our basic needs. We cannot feed our own starvation-level civilians let alone support the millions of extra men we need to undertake an invasion of fortress Europe. The lifeline will soon be withdrawn if American troopships are sunk, with the almost inevitable loss of all passengers in transit across the Atlantic. We MUST find ways of surmounting the Atlantic problem, and find it quickly.

Air cover in mid-Atlantic is non-existent. Coastal Command and the U.S. Coastguard can provide air cover only on the fringes of the Atlantic within about 600 miles of their bases. In the 500mile gap in the middle the U-boats have almost complete freedom to operate, freedom to surface and recharge their batteries and to communicate by radio with their brother wolves, with Admiral

Doenitz back at base and with long-range Focke Wulf 'Kondor', aircraft scouting for convoys. U-boat commanders can conduct their navigational sextant-shots without interference. They can manoeuvre into attack positions on the surface at seventeen knots instead of being limited to the absolute maximum of six knots, for a very short time, imposed by battery propulsion when submerged. With so much accurate information and manoeuvrability they find it easy to be lying in wait with a pack of ten or more boats right in the path of convoys plodding along at anything between three and twelve knots. They take their pick of the victims, run the gauntlet of the pitifully small escorting force, attack, stay submerged to pick off stragglers and wait until the rearguard has moved on. They then come up to the surface, go full speed ahead to outflank the convoy and get ahead again to submerge and repeat the operation. This can go on for many consecutive days and nights. U-boat commanders become record-breaking heroes on every trip, with freshly painted success symbols on their conning towers and a brass-band welcome on their return to Lorient, the massive complex of reinforced concrete U-boat pens on the west coast of France.

The Allied convoy surface Escort usually consists of five corvettes with one frigate commanded by the Senior Officer of the Escort (SoE). To date, the biggest convoy between Halifax and the U.K. has been eighty-three ships, although some senior officers consider that the optimum for North Atlantic conditions is nearer to forty five. Shepherding so many assorted vessels with varying degrees of manoeuvrability, reliability, speed and polyglot crews, all condemned to sail at the speed of the slowest, is a thankless task.

A broad front to the convoy is preferred with a small number of ships in a column so that, faced with a submerged attack, the sooner ships get past the submarine the less the exposure to danger. For the same reason we try to keep station 400 yards astern of each other in the columns but as more and more inexperienced watch keepers are recruited this must be increased, probably to 800 yards. Between columns 600 yards by day and 1000 yards by night has been the norm, but many Commodores are adopting 1000 yards as standard, on the principle that it offers a more open target. Also, having it fixed avoids the traffic chaos at dawn and dusk when convoy columns have to open out or close in during the half-light of those periods. The outside line of a ten-column convoy opening up by 400 yards per file has to move sideways by 1800 yards. This is still the case when the convoy can include an old tramp vessel, which can barely keep up with a slow four knot convoy. It can take four hours flat out to take up the new station, twice a day, which causes many an old engine to disintegrate. What does an S.O.E. do with a broken down hulk in mid-Atlantic? Abandon it? Lose one of his escort vessels to tow it to safety thus risking the hazards of the tow for perhaps 1200 miles, at the same time jeopardising the whole convoy by reducing escort cover? The hard decision to be made depends upon her cargo. If carrying useless deadweight as ballast, for stability, as so often is the case when western bound because we have so little to export, then he takes off her crew and scuttles her. Such responsibility makes young men old and hardens old men into iron.

A convoy consisting of forty ships, therefore, in ten columns of four ships each will cover an area of 9000 yards by 2800 yards assuming a ship length of one hundred yards and absolutely perfect station-keeping, which is quite impossible. Remembering that visibility in winter and at night in the North Atlantic is usually low to non-existent, the task of the Escort is difficult, to say the least. Every alarm, real or false, has to be followed up and investigated at the maximum speed compatible with the prevailing sea conditions, resulting in these tiny corvettes taking seas over the bows, rolling gunwales under, or both. The miseries of flooded living quarters, bruised or broken limbs, being deprived of hot meals and hot drinks by the quenching of galley stoves, wet and mildewed clothes without any hope of getting them dried, howling gales, snow and ice, cutting winds and frostbite are torments to the crews. The worse the conditions, the longer they have to be endured when progress is slow. For the corvette captain, every alarm and excursion means dangerously high consumption of meagre supplies of precious bunker fuel, with the unthinkable risk of running out and being at the mercy of the elements and the enemy.

The ability of a U-boat to attack, night after night, a convoy which has no airborne protection, is paying huge dividends to the enemy. We are losing as many as 20% of convoyed ships in a single crossing. How long can we survive? Cargoes resting on the seabed are of no use to the armed forces and civilians desperately awaiting delivery in the U.K. We are losing ships much faster than we can build them and the Merchant Navy personnel who die are beyond value and completely irreplaceable. Do you know what value the shipping industry placed upon our merchant seamen at that time? The instant a ship is sunk the wages of the crew are stopped, dead or alive. No matter how many days survivors may spend in open boats, they get no pay. It is obscene that ship owners enjoy the lifestyle they have, but this is because so many of the Great British Public don't know and don't care as long as they get their rations.

Enemy shipyards, in spite of RAF bombing, are still sending twenty new U-boats to join the wolf packs every month. Some of them are their new supply submarines, the "milch-kuhs" with a surface displacement of around 2000 tons which enables them to ferry fuel, food, (including fresh meat, bread and vegetables so important to the health, morale and efficiency of the wolf pack crews) and extra torpedoes. These replenishments will increase the effectiveness of the packs enormously by increasing the ratio of their time on station to total passage time. The new U-boats are equipped with an anti-radar detector of French design called "Metox". This gives them early warning of the approach of our "Air to Surface Vessel" (A.S.V.) Radar, giving them time to submerge or to man their recently and massively increased anti-aircraft armament and fight it out on the surface. We had hoped until now that we would be receiving great numbers of American-built Escort Carriers but naturally, with their entry into hostilities, their own need is seen by them to be greater than ours. Of the limited number we have received none has yet gone into active service because of conflict of specification. We are worried about their wooden decks, the safety of the magazines, electrical installations and their aviation spirit storage and distribution systems. That our worries are justified is borne out by the American built H.M.S. Dasher's self-destruction by explosion, killing 378 of her crew. Modification to these factors is taking up valuable time and shipyard capacity, while there is an urgent need for the carrier escorts at sea. Can we divert R.A.F. long-range heavy bombers from our offensive on German industry to help us achieve air supremacy over our convoys? That is unthinkable, because the whole of the enemy war effort would be given a breathing space, which could prove to be a winner for them, with failure and eventual defeat for us. The implication is that we are losing the Battle of the Atlantic, but we can't contemplate that! Where will it all end? What are we going to do about it? We must first consider what we would LIKE to do about it and then in true British fashion reach a compromise about the reality of what is possible.

We need enough aircraft carriers to provide continuous air cover as part of every convoy and we need them tomorrow. They should carry at least six planes, some of them anti-submarine and some fighters to strafe the new generation of' U-boats equipped to fight it out on the surface. They should have a flight deck 500 feet long, a width (inboard of the bridge) of 70 to 80 feet and a speed of 15 knots, say 18,000 gross registered tons, and a hangar to hold all the aircraft and still allow room for working on spread wings when necessary. They must have a safe magazine for rockets, depth charges, bombs, ammunition and pyrotechnics, together with tankage for 10,000 gallons of aviation petrol and safe distribution facilities for dispensing it in the hangar or on deck. At least one lift is required between hangar and deck for aircraft maintenance, storage and operation. There must be a bridge structure conducive to good navigation and manoeuvrability in aircraft carrier duties in convoy. It must also give minimal interference with aircraft operation yet minimal outboard overhang, so that the vessel can use commercial shore installations and berths without damage to herself or dockside equipment. To avoid disruption to flying and deck-handling personnel, engine exhaust gases and smoke must be suitably diverted below deck level and downwind. There should be the facility to carry cargo with minimal reduction in capacity and the ability to load and discharge cargo simply, without huge deck access to holds, at top speed for rapid convoy turnround and without encroaching on aircraft carrier requirements. Since cargo carrying is involved, the ship must be in the defensive rôle and be operated by the Merchant Navy under the Red Ensign.

Accommodation will be required for substantial numbers of Defensively Equipped Merchant Ship (DEMS) gunners of the Royal Artillery, to man the large number of 20 mm Oerlikon and 40 mm Bofors anti-aircraft guns necessary to defend a Merchant Aircraft Carrier (Macship) in addition to the four inch stern gun which is fairly standard on all merchant ships over 2000 tons. Fleet Air Arm aircrews, ground crew, Air Staff Officer, medical personnel, extra galley staff and stewards all need living space. It is most unlikely that anything is available to fit the bill and it would seem that we shall have to build from scratch to get what we want.

Investigation of this route shows that all shipyard capacity for vessels of 12,000 tons or over is already occupied or irrevocably committed. Another blind alley! Must we go for smaller ships; should we commandeer hulls already on the stocks early enough to incorporate our modified specification; or should we take over existing ships which can be altered to our reduced requirements? Because of the desperate urgency, we must use all of these less-than-perfect choices. We cannot have access to any of the conventional Naval dockyard capacity and the Macship concept will have to come under the jurisdiction and control of the Admiralty Merchant Shipping Department.

Grain-carrying ships and oil tankers are the only existing vessels, which meet our cargo criteria, allowing cargo to be pumped or blown to load and unload. However they are below 12,000 tons, so some limitations are inevitably forced upon us. Shipyards experienced only in building merchant ships of dimensions up to and including the "standard tramp vessel" will have to be used.

The Naval Staff Committee have debated all the modifications necessary to convert a "standard tramp" hull into an operational Macship and despite difficulties and disagreements have approved a revised and compromised specification. What the operational aircrews will think of a flight deck "not less than" three hundred and ninety feet long and sixty two feet wide and a speed "in fair weather" of eleven knots remains to be heard, but at this stage we are not in a position to let them know of our agreement. It is sufficient to say that this is the smallest deck-landing aircraft carrier ever built or likely to be built in the future. The single-engine, open cockpit, three-man "Swordfish" biplane is the only aircraft which will cope with Macship limitations, carry a sufficient load of anti-submarine armament and be robust enough to survive the difficult landings it will experience. One hold will be made available on grain ships to convert into a hangar to hold four Swordfish but, on tankers, aircraft will have to remain on deck at the mercy of the elements at all times. The ground crews who maintain them will experience conditions, which no human being should be expected to endure. Future generations, brought up on "Health and Safety at Work" directives will never understand the spirit of devotion to duty which conditions men to stretch themselves to the limit, for the sake of people who willingly put their lives at stake for a common cause. Without a hangar, tanker Macships will be limited to three Swordfish because of restrictions to take-off caused by aircraft parked aft, and to landing by aircraft parked on the bow. Three planes weighing four tons each will have to be manhandled up and down a pitching, rolling and oily deck to allow clearance for takeoff and landing to take place. An aeroplane returning from a long patrol with little petrol left can't cruise around for long, while an unserviceable aircraft is made ready to be moved, so physical exertion is going to be pitted against the clock.

We hope that the decision makers have the practical experience to qualify them to take such vital considerations into their assessment of what is, and what is not, an acceptable specification. God help the Macship crews if they are wrong. On the other hand, God help the Merchant Navy if they don't get air cover soon.

Whether the decision makers are right or wrong, orders are now placed for two Macships of the grain ship type at the Burntisland Shipbuilding Co. Ltd. and within a fortnight this is increased to six, by ordering two from Wm. Denny Bros. Ltd. and two from Lithgows Ltd. Each grain-carrier Macship will operate a flight of four Swordfish (from a hangar converted from a grain-hold) to provide the long-awaited air cover. The conception is over and the gestation has started.

Chapter Three

Aircraft Carriers in Miniature

The first grain-carrier Macship, *Empire MacAlpine*, ordered in June 1942, had her keel laid on August 11th, 1942, was launched December 23rd, 1942, and was handed over with completed inspection and trials on April 21st, 1943. During this time work on the oil tanker concept was pressing ahead but it was slowed by our overwhelming need for oil and the U-boat predilection for tankers as targets. In October 1942 it was decided to convert nine existing tankers belonging to the Anglo-Saxon Petroleum Co. Ltd., all of much the same dimensions and of a similar class, each to operate a flight of three Swordfish from a deck open to the elements without the benefit of a hangar. By ingenious design and full co-operation between Anglo-Saxon Petroleum, Messrs Palmers, Hebburn Co. Ltd., and Smiths Dock Co. Ltd., more than half the 1,000 tons of steelwork in the conversion could be prefabricated, so reducing cost and reducing time on the slipways in the shipyards. At the same time four new tanker Macships were ordered from Messrs. Harland and Wolff Ltd., Cammell Laird & Co. Ltd., and the two yards of Swan Hunter & Wigham Richardson Ltd. Deliveries were planned to commence in April 1943 and to be complete by October 1943. They started on time and some were then delayed by problems in manufacture of arrester wires and hangar lifts. The nineteenth and final delivery came in April 1944.

The Fleet Air Arm Macship Wing, consisting of 836 Naval Air Squadron and 860 Royal Netherlands Naval Air Squadron, was created to provide the aviation requirements of all nineteen ships. Two oil tanker Macs were allocated to the Dutchmen who manned two flights and the remaining eleven tankers and six grain-ship Macs, were looked after by twenty-three flights created within 836 Squadron. This arrangement made 836 the biggest squadron of all time and it has held the record into the twenty-first century, as, in the course of its life, it grew to hold over one hundred Swordfish and ninety crews each composed of pilot, observer and telegraphist-air-gunner. Initially the Royal Naval Air Station at Machrihanish, on Kintyre, was allocated to be the base for the Wing, but this location, although ideally accessible from seawards, involved a tiresome road journey for supplies and personnel from Glasgow along narrow and twisting roads. Transfer to Maydown near to Londonderry in Northern Ireland was some improvement, though not for personnel because of the Larne to Stranraer, Heysham to Belfast or Glasgow to Belfast ferry crossings, which were always overcrowded. They were also unpredictable and uncomfortable due to the difficult and treacherous sea crossing. Since home leave was not even contemplated this part of the pros and cons didn't even enter into the equation. Proximity to the Anti-Submarine School at Londonderry contributed much more weight to the decision. A similar support base was needed across the Atlantic and, with the cooperation of the Royal Canadian Air Force this was established at Dartmouth, Nova Scotia, next door to the huge safe harbour at Halifax.

The first Macship to come into service was the *Empire MacAlpine*. She was brought from Burntisland, round the north of Scotland to the Clyde Estuary where, under sheltered conditions, she could start to weld together the miscellany presented to her as an embryo ship's company. The Macship herself, fell far short of anyone's concept of what was needed for the task ahead. She was too short, too narrow, too small, too light, too slow and with too much top hamper too high up.

However she had one overwhelming advantage, which was that everyone concerned was glad to see her, in spite of her shortcomings.

There were three weeks available before it was essential for *Empire MacAlpine* to sail as an efficient protector of a Halifax-bound convoy, and there was so much to be learnt, practised and perfected in a multiplicity of skills as yet unknown. A complement of about one hundred and ten consisted of the usual 40 Merchant Navy Officers and crew manning this size of grain ship, plus the extra staff required to cope with the nearly-tripled number of souls aboard and the new function, aviation. The extras were Merchant Navy catering staff and stewards, Fleet Air Arm aircrew, aircraft maintenance and deck handling parties, extra communications, liaison and medical staff, and a large number of Defensibly Equipped Merchant Ship (DEMS) personnel from the Royal Artillery. The Commanding Officer of 836 Squadron, Lieutenant Commander Ransford Slater O.B.E., D.S.C., R.N. carried out the first deck landing on *Empire MacAlpine*, on May 7th, 1943, and coordinated the intensive training of the ship's company in all aspects of the flying function. The results achieved were little short of miraculous and were mainly due to the terrific goodwill, which came from every direction. The aircrew admired the way the Master handled his ship to give the best possible conditions and position for landing and take-off. He, in turn admired the deck handlers who spread and folded wings so rapidly, ranging the Swordfish for flight or striking them down into the hangar, without prolonging the time that the ship had to sail into wind, on a course other than that of the convoy. This would reduce exposure of the ship to attack, especially when the wind was from astern and the ship was heading away from the shelter of the convoy lanes. The result was that, whenever flying took place, every off-duty person would gather in the shelter of the netted-off safety gangways on both sides of the flight-deck, and then leap out to help the deck handling party to speed things up, reducing the back-breaking work and at the same time shortening the duration of exposure to danger. Sharing such voluntary tasks forged many bonds of friendship between the different Services. The Chief Engineer took it upon himself to leave the engine-room responsibility to his deputy, in order to operate the arrester wires and to be present, in the event of an accident, to take charge and save seconds with his knowledge of the mechanics of moving machinery, which could be applied to tangled wreckage.

During the work-up, the aircrews developed trust in each other, as pilots gained confidence in their own ability to fly to and from the smallest carrier in the world, and in the competence of the Deck Landing Control Officer to guide and control them on their approach and landing, albeit under ideal conditions, in very sheltered waters. Navigational exercises strengthened the faith of Pilot and Telegraphist air-gunner in their Observer's ability to know where North is, Many navigational exercises were carried out by aircrew to determine wind speed and direction over water, because the prospect of their lives being dependent upon dead reckoning navigation, with radio and radar silence, demanded second-nature accuracy in this task.

Many depth charges were dropped and rounds of ammunition fired, and after each depth charge, a lifeboat would be launched, nominally for boat-drill, but in reality to collect fresh fish for dinner.

At the end of each exhausting day the deck handling crew lowered the last Swordfish into the hangar and made all secure There was no rest for the aircraft maintenance crew, who, as a foretaste of the future, had to refuel, correct any malfunctions of engine, airframe, radio, electrics or instruments and ensure that the plane was fully operational before signing Form 700 to that effect, for the pilot's acceptance before the next take-off.

Having achieved in three weeks what would have taken months in R.N. peacetime conditions lacking in urgency, *Empire MacAlpine* and her united Ship's Company were, in the time-honoured phrase, " ready in all respects for sea" and on May 29th, 1943, they joined a convoy out of Liverpool westward-bound for Halifax.

It is a great pity that so much time was lost in initiating the construction of Macships; because our monthly losses of merchant ships in the winter of1942/3 were appalling. This was largely due to the withdrawal of escort vessels for use in the "Operation Torch" landings in North Africa, and the ferocity of the winter gales, which reduced the efficiency of the remaining escorts and increased their time in dock. The strength of the U-boat fleet had grown to 331 in the second half of 1942, and Doenitz used his increased force to his best advantage in the Atlantic Gap with the benefit of xB-dienst deciphering machinery which broke the code of Royal Navy messages giving convoy position reports. The Escort Carriers coming into service, were not available in the Atlantic as they, too, had been diverted to "Operation Torch." The U-boat initiative was supported by the use of nine milch cow submarines conveying huge amounts of replenishments to U-boats out on patrol, thus increasing their ratio of offensive time to total time at sea.

In the nine months before the first Macship escorted an Atlantic convoy, 362 merchantmen were sunk by U-boats. The number sunk in the following nine months was 61, but *only two ships were sunk in all the convoys escorted by a macship in spite of the fact that there were more and better U-boats in the North Atlantic at the end of the European War than at the peak of the Battle of the Atlantic.* The catastrophic effect of earlier failure to provide close round-the-clock air cover for every convoy, was about to be exposed.

Oil Tanker MV. *Alexia* before conversion to a Merchant Aircraft Carrier

Macship MV. *Alexia* after conversion from a standard
Oil Tanker, still carrying 95% of her original cargo of oil

Amastra with palisades erected; the only shelter from
Atlantic fury for aircraft and men. *Alexia* and *Amastra*
were sister ships of the *Rapana* class of oil-tanker Macships

My second ship, the oil tanker Macship, *Empire MacColl*

Chapter Four

The Fledgling

What kind of a person was needed to be the pilot of a Swordfish flying from a Macship?   The author illustrates his background and experiences in training for this hazardous job.

Born on the 11th July 1923, I was seven weeks over my sixteenth birthday when war was declared on 3rd September 1939. My matriculation examination results came through on the day before war broke out and I was faced with a dilemma: whether to accept the County Exhibition which had been awarded to me on the basis of Distinctions in Maths, Physics and Chemistry and Credits in seven other subjects, to enable me to stay on to go to University; or to leave school, go into industry and study at night school to get a London external degree. Having seen at first hand the effect that unemployment had on able and intelligent people in the slump years of the 1926 to 1938 period in the Tees-side area, and thinking that the war might last about three or four years I chose to avoid the easy option of full-time education, in case I would graduate but have no practical experience at the beginning of a massive world slump, which I expected would automatically follow the end of the war. I applied to Imperial Chemical Industries (Fertilisers and Synthetic Products) Ltd., for a post as Research Assistant at Billingham-on-Tees, to be told that all recruitment was suspended until further notice. While it was not put into words there was the implication "Don't you know there is a war on?"

Having turned down my academic prospects, I now had to find some work to keep the wolf from the door. A stop-gap job in the office of the Personnel Manager at Smiths Dock, South Bank, Middlesbrough, calculating wages of the dockyard workers, gave me an insight into the low value placed on unskilled labour, and the narrow margin between them and the skilled tradesman who had served his apprenticeship. The rate for a craftsman fitter or turner was one shilling an hour for a 52 hour week, amounting to Two

Pounds and Twelve Shillings per week (£2.60), whereas an unskilled labourer earned nine pence an hour for the same number of hours amounting to One pound and Nineteen Shillings per week (£1.95). From these sums there were deductions for Tax, National Insurance, Unemployment Benefit, and Union dues. Pay-day on Friday brought many wives to the Dockyard gates in an attempt to secure their husbands' pay, before it was irretrievably passed over a bar into the eagerly waiting hands of a publican. They were hard times for the families of irresponsible men.

After six weeks, I saw an advertisement for a laboratory assistant at British Titan Products Ltd., manufacturers of Titanium Oxide as a base for paint. I applied for, and was given the job of testing samples of Titanium Oxide, making them up into paint and exposing them to simulated severe weather conditions to test their quality. To my extreme embarrassment, after a further fortnight Imperial Chemical Industries wrote to me offering an interview for a post as Research Assistant and I accepted this and started work as a probationer under training in the Analytical Laboratory on December 1st 1939, at the princely salary of £55 per annum.

My first month's salary was to teach me a lesson in later life. After tax, insurance and "stamps", I was left with three pounds and fifteen shillings, (£3.75), which I dutifully offered to my mother. Father intervened and suggested that I should invest it in War Savings Certificates, which I duly did. It purchased five certificates at fifteen shillings each, redeemable in five years at one pound each. At the time of purchase, the money would have bought me two suits at the Thirty Shilling Tailors and a pair of all-leather shoes. On redemption, five pounds would buy two suits at the (now) Fifty Shilling Tailors leaving nothing towards a pair of shoes.

The "Phoney War" came and went, leaving the nation shocked and reeling with the reality of defeat in Holland, Belgium, and France, but with thankfulness for the miracle of Dunkirk and the return of family, friends and neighbours, lucky enough to escape from the overwhelming power of the German war machine. My brother Bob, who had patriotically volunteered for the Territorial Army at the time of Munich in 1938, had been called up two days before war was declared. He was immediately sent to France with the British Expeditionary Force and with little more than open Bren-gun carriers, first-war Lee-Enfield rifles and a five round clip of .303 ins. ammunition. He had advanced up into Belgium until his unit met Panzer Divisions and was compelled to fall back to Dunkirk, where he stayed on the beaches. He joined up with a rearguard destroying abandoned guns, vehicles and equipment until days after Churchill announced that the evacuation of Dunkirk was complete. Several nights later, Bob was taken off the beach under cover of darkness by the destroyer H.M.S. 'Shikari', which was doing a last-minute sweep to pick up survivors and rearguard defenders.

How unimportant seemed my efforts, (and how difficult to concentrate) at the Constantine Technical College, three hours a night, three nights a week after a nine-hour day at work. I was planning to take an external London University Bachelor of Science degree, reading Maths, Physics and Chemistry to be followed, by an Honours degree in Chemistry. The war was suddenly very real, with visions of a triumphant Wehrmacht, rampaging through our towns and villages as they had on the Continent. We could imagine all the distress and horrors faced by a displaced civilian population, young and old, sick and infirm, homeless and aimlessly wandering the roads, hungry and harassed.

The formation of the Local Defence Volunteers was a rallying point for all able-bodied men and, though I was still sixteen and the lower limit was seventeen, no-one was inclined to ask questions. In the absence of any arms except some 1914-8 bayonets, one of my first jobs was to salvage copper wire from some old electric cable and use it to bind bayonets to broom handles. A veteran of the Spanish Civil War who was now a shop steward on the railway inspired us to start making " Molotov Cocktails", which were bottles filled with any inflammable liquid and with a plug of rag stuffed into the neck. In theory one took up a position behind a wall or in an upper storey, waiting for a tank to come along with an open hatch. When such a target presented itself, one struck a match and ignited the rag then threw the missile into the tank, where the glass would shatter and the contents ignite. The tank crew in their hurry to get out were, theoretically, vulnerable targets. However, the veteran admitted that striking matches in the face of an oncoming tank made one a vulnerable target also, and, since this target always had to appear before the tank crew were exposed, the odds were in favour of the tank crew. This gave me an idea.

When clearing out a cupboard in the analytical laboratory, I had come across a glass container, which held about 500 grams of yellow phosphorus immersed in paraffin, thus excluding the oxygen needed to initiate combustion. Unable to think of a way to dispose of it, I had replaced it where the cobwebs had grown to almost hide it. Why not use the phosphorus to act as the igniter in a Molotov Cocktail? A hazelnut-sized piece of phosphorous in a bottle of flammable liquid should do the trick. With paraffin it was a failure, as twenty minutes could elapse after breakage before oxygen could get to the phosphorus to let it ignite. We needed a much more volatile and flammable fluid. Although petrol was scarce, volunteers produced two gallons in total and I went into production. This was a hazardous procedure, involving the speedy transfer of a pre-cut piece of phosphorus into a bottle filled to the top with petrol. A crown cork was then crimped to the neck of the bottle by means of a blow by a mallet to a tapered collet placed over the crown cork. Fifty cocktails were produced in this way, surprisingly, without mishap. Two were used in proving the functioning of the weapon, which ignited within five seconds of smashing the bottle, and forty-eight were cached in sixes under the floorboards in the bedrooms of eight volunteers. These hiding places expanded to accommodate any ammunition my friends and I could acquire, by fair means or foul, as long as the threat of invasion existed. We intended to sell our lives dearly. By the time I went into the Fleet Air Arm my hoard included twenty-four Mills hand grenades (with fuses stored separately) and 180 rounds of .300 inch calibre ammunition for Ross rifles or our Lease-Lend Lewis machine gun. Although we may have been figures of fun as "Dad's Army" we intended to occupy the attentions of a considerable number of the invading forces. We even begged some scrapped steel plates from the local shipyard and used them to armour a railway truck and a 1905 tank-engine, with the intention of sabotaging the swing bridge at the entrance to Middlesbrough Docks, possibly under fire. Our platoon had a high proportion of London and North Eastern Railway employees who were platelayers or signalmen so we had a fund of local knowledge, which would enable us to create mayhem by organising pile-ups at critical points. Hitler's decision to abandon invasion saved many of my generation from suicide missions.

The Luftwaffe adopted a policy of intrusion into northern airspace, which would cause the maximum of interruption to industry and the greatest disturbance to the comfort and welfare of the civilian population. They spread their attacks thinly over as wide an area as possible so that Air Raid Warnings were widespread and of long duration, keeping workers out of their beds and under stress so that their efficiency at work next day would be minimal. The blast furnaces of Cargo Fleet and Dorman Long on Tees-side were kept in suspense and indecision to tap a furnace, an operation that lit up the whole sky with a brilliant glow, which could be seen as far as thirty miles away. Molten slag drawn off a furnace into huge cast iron tipping rail-trucks, had to be tipped on slagheaps whilst still molten. If allowed to cool it set solid in the truck, and then that truck had to be scrapped. Intruding Junker 88s, Heinkel 111s and Messerschmitt 110s were on the lookout for such tempting targets and once my unit received a Lease-Lend, World War One, .300 inch calibre Lewis machine gun my hope and ambition was to shoot down one of these planes on his run-in to bomb a blast furnace. To that end, I spent hours in a blacked-out room taking apart and reassembling the Lewis gun by feel, and simulating various stoppages and how to free the gun and get it back into action. In this way I got to know every component and its function. I was given the single chevron of a Lance Corporal and at the mature age of seventeen, was put in charge of the Platoon's machine gun section. My subsequent request for an anti-aircraft mounting for the gun met with the reply that these were not available and unlikely to become available in the foreseeable future. It was recommended that a guard of suitable stature should secure his steel helmet on his head as firmly as possible, stand rigidly to attention, and the two forelegs of the Lewis gun should then be rested one each side of the helmet, standing on the brim. Since dental hygiene was of a generally poor standard amongst artisans in those days I was rather afraid that we might rattle the teeth out of our prop man, so I sent out search parties for scrap angle-iron and ended up with two bedsteads which were converted into a tripod mounting by dint of much laborious hand sawing, drilling and bolting. It served its purpose well, but Jerry flew on unscathed and probably un-frightened.

My new responsibilities were a mixed blessing. Previously the twelve-hour guard-duty, which we had to do once every week, enabled me to get some sleep in the form of two-hour cat-naps between sentry duties, but now, every time the sky lit up, I had to be out there behind my pride and joy. Without tracer rounds shooting at night was not so much a case of hit and miss, as miss, miss, and miss. My ammunition hoard increased every time a Lewis rotary ammunition pan had to be changed. They held forty-seven rounds but fired so fast that no-one could count them. I salved my conscience by thinking that one active partisan was worth ten dead Home Guards and filched one round from each pan to add to my hoard.

Pressures continued to grow and during term time my week was allocated as follows:

		Hours per week
ICI	Mon-Fri 8.00 to 5.30, half-hour lunch, 5x9hrs	45
	Sat 8.00 to 1.00	5
	Fire-watch duty one night per week 6pm to 6am	12
Home Guard	Training parades 2 nights 7 to 9 pm	4
	Sunday 9 to 12 am	3
	Guard duty;- one all-night 6pm to 6 am	12
	Field day;- 8 hrs once per month	2
Nightschool	Tues Wed Thurs: 6.30 to 9.30 pm	9
	Set homework	6
Travelling	Mon-Sat: Two and a half hours per day	15
	Sunday	1
	Total	114
		Hours per week

Air raids disrupted the time remaining for sleep and recreation but these were so variable and unpredictable that no attempt has been made to evaluate their effect. Suffice it to say that coming on top of an exhausting workload their effect was devastating. My love for my parents was paramount yet I recall with shame my reaction to my father's call for me to "wake up and come on down to the shelter" shortly after I had fallen into exhausted sleep. Even though I was aware that he stood guard over me and never called me until he could actually hear aircraft, bombs dropping, or anti-aircraft fire opening up, I retorted "for God's sake leave me alone and go on down to your funk-hole". How that must have hurt a man as brave as my Dad, who went through the first-world-war and was twice Mentioned in Despatches. I would give anything to be able to rectify that injustice. The intolerable and prolonged stress I was experiencing was no excuse. My ability to cat-nap was developed by constant practice but my ability to achieve instant alertness on awakening was not so highly developed.

The recorded travelling time was mainly by push-bike, a single speed twenty-year-old veteran discarded by my grandfather after my grandmother persuaded him that it was unsafe to be ridden on the road. I inherited it at the age of seven on condition that I stripped it down to its basic components, discarded any faulty or worn parts and replaced them using the birthday and Christmas financial aid of the whole family. I finally reassembled the whole to the satisfaction of Grand-dad, Dad, Uncle Stan, brother Bob, various courtiers of my many aunts and any other interested member of our extended family. In the course of this tuition I learned how to retain ball-bearings in a ball-race, using a bed of Vaseline, how to adjust a ball-race and a brake setting, and which way to mount brake shoes so that the direction of wheel rotation did not eject brake blocks on application. I also learned how to grind an old file into a draw-scraper to remove old enamel down to the bare metal of the frame then to use a blowlamp to dry and heat the metal for the application of black stove enamel. My family took pride in passing on this kind of practical knowledge yet at the same time they got me to reason out my own solution to a problem. Excellent training for a seven-year old!

In 1940, the twelve miles each way between South Bank, where I lived, and Hartburn, the village to which I.C.I. had evacuated our research laboratory, crossed the centre of Middlesbrough and then took the "wilderness" route to Stockton, a bleak four mile open and straight road offering no shelter whatever to cyclists across the river plain. It was wonderful when the wind came from behind but a torment when it came from ahead, without my having the benefit of the choice of gears. The alternative to this was to travel by bus which was not attractive as it was a half-hourly service without bus shelters which ran erratically because of wartime shortages of maintenance staff, spares, drivers and conductresses. Another disadvantage was that on a bus I always fell asleep and could easily go a long way past my destination. After night school, going home meant catching the last bus at 9.35 pm from Middlesbrough, which terminated at Saltburn ten miles beyond home. Several times I was awakened at the Saltburn bus garage at about 10.30 pm and faced with the prospect of a two-and-a-half hour walk home in the black-out and perhaps in rain, or to plead with the night watchman to be allowed to kip down on the long side-seat of a double-decker bus. Unfortunately, in those days none of our family, friends or neighbours had a telephone and there was no means of letting Mother know what had happened to me and to save her the worry I walked, except on one occasion when it was snowing and it could be assumed that I had stayed at work.

On one night in the spring of 1941, when I had chosen to use the bus to go home after night school, a stick of six bombs was dropped on Middlesbrough Road, South Bank, the first one about a hundred yards in front of the bus. Amidst a shower of debris and an ear-thumping shockwave, our bus slewed to a halt and I fell off the platform where I had been standing in anticipation of getting off at my stop. By the time I picked myself up and took stock of the situation, screams and shouts could be heard from what was left of a terrace of three-storey houses, with cellars. These had been built at the beginning of the century for middle class shop-owners, who could afford a couple of maids to live-in up in the attic level, but were now overcrowded with many generations of artisans.

Fortunately for the occupants who survived the bomb-blast there was a massive chimneybreast structure between each pair of houses, connecting the maze of chimney ducts necessary to serve all the fire-hearths required to take the chill off high, draughty rooms. Generously dimensioned floor joists, which remained embedded in the chimneybreast, but were dislodged at their far end, formed a support for rubble and gave a haven of protection underneath. It was along such tunnels that the locals and I tried to work towards the cries and screams coming so pitifully from inside the rubble. To our horror, there were explosions as pockets of gas from ruptured mains were ignited either by sparks from mangled electrical circuits or from scattered embers from fire-grates. Broken pipes were leaking water, but thankfully at a dribbling rate due to the extent of the bomb damage to the local water grid. Dozens of people who were trapped in their cellars by debris, watched the water rise while they shouted for help, guessing how long it would be before they would be rescued. Hours later, one such survivor said to me that in the docks they caught rats in cages with a gate which dropped behind the rat on entrance and cut off its escape. His method of disposal of the caged, live rat was to drop the cage, weighted with a brick and tied on the end of a rope, into the river until the rat's struggles ceased. "Never again" he vowed, with a shudder.

The only light I had was a pocket torch, with a partly obscured lens, which we all carried during those days of total blackout. The batteries were on the point of exhaustion and replacements almost impossible to obtain. Shopping around next day I was told "Don't you know there's a war on?" I had to give up my solo rescue work after a couple of hours when the faint light died away at last, but not before I got an old man out from beside his ground floor fireside. He had been left tucked up in his armchair smoking his pipe, being too fragile to go down into the cellar. After handing him over to the Salvation Army Survivor Support Team, I gratefully accepted the British panacea for all ills, a mug of strong tea. After enjoying it, I went back to see how my old man was after his ordeal, to find he had eluded his carers and disappeared. Remembering his stress at the loss of his treasured pipe I looked into the hole from which he had been extracted and found him " just looking for my pipe".

Another picture of that night, etched indelibly in my memory is of a rescuer, carrying the body of a two or three-year-old girl, with tears channelling unashamedly down his begrimed face, repeating over and over again "The bastards, the lousy rotten stinking bastards." It was then that the horror of the mess we were in swept over me. That same rescuer would be proud to call for a pint of beer for a hero in RAF uniform who had bombed Germany the night before. My intention to volunteer for flying duties in the Fleet Air Arm rather than the R.A.F. hardened because my war was against armed men who could hit back, not old men, women and children, however much they supported their national war effort.

The thought of pressing a bomb-release over civilian occupied areas was abhorrent and would put me on the same level as our enemy. I did not have the guts to contribute to our war effort in the way that Bomber Command did and I know we would have lost the war without them.

I left the bombed site to the professionals and the trained amateurs and made my weary way home to my worried but immensely relieved parents, stopping on the way to pick up my rucksack of books and my raincoat which I had dropped on the pavement when I fell off the bus a lifetime before. That it was still there caused me no surprise. A sign of the times? Mother prepared a bath for me in the scullery and took away my one and only suit to try to repair the ravages of the night. I got into bed at about four am for three hours of sleep, broken by nightmares of the worst moments of the night and the creaking and groaning of the settling debris. Next day I resolved to be at the door of the recruiting office at nine am on July 11th of that year, 1941, my eighteenth birthday.

And so I was. The recruiting Master-at-Arms paternally questioned my determination to join up when I was in a reserved occupation. He tackled me with some very probing questions, which let me know that he suspected that I was in trouble with the irate father of some poor little pregnant girl, or that I faced imminent exposure for embezzlement of a huge sum of money. Eventually he passed me on to the next stage of selection, which was an interview by a board of examiners consisting of Naval Officers ranking from a Lieutenant Commander to a Commodore. The interview was to be held at Darlington ten days hence, at 9 am. necessitating a day off work, to the grave displeasure of my Senior-staff manager to whom I had to disclose my intention to join H.M. Forces. His reaction was what I would have expected had I intended to join I.G. Farben Industrie in Düsseldorf taking as much I.C.I. confidential documentation with me as I could lay my hands on. I was disloyal, immature, self-seeking, unreliable and ungrateful for all the wonderful opportunities I had been given during my training. Did I not realise that if I persisted in my stupidity, there would come a day when, cap in hand, I would be asking for my job back from ex-colleagues who would have acquired seniority, experience and salary advantage whilst I played at being a Naval Aviator acquiring skills which no-one would want in peace-time. Though he could not prevent me from obeying an Admiralty instruction, my disloyalty would be noted on my records. As he was both a communist and Jewish, I never understood why he disapproved of someone wanting to fight Fascism.

The medical examination was pretty thorough, but presented only one problem. I had been worried about my eyesight as one eye was excellent for long distance whilst the other was perfect for close-up work. However I was kept sitting naked in a draughty corridor for about twenty minutes and whiled away the time by learning the bottom line of an optician's chart, backwards and forwards as I could see it through an open door. When it came to the test, I could read the second from bottom line and then quote the bottom line from memory. During my training, my eyesight was never a problem, in fact an abnormally dilating pupil was a big advantage when night-vision was required, as it was when I was later remustered as a night-fighter pilot. My major practical problem during the medical was experienced, however, when given a hundred ml. container, in which to submit a sample of urine. To strangle the flow in mid-stream after hanging about for ages in the nude and subjected to draughts, demanded great concentration. My cup was full and overflowing.

Dressed again, I was sent into the interview room and seated on a lone chair in front of a naval battleline poised to send in its destroyers to beat its opponent into submission without any damage to itself. I was intimidated by the high-ranking gold braid, until it came to answering mental arithmetic questions. "You cycle from A to B into a headwind at ten miles per hour, and return downwind at fifteen miles an hour. What is your average speed?" This was right up my street and I gave the correct answer of twelve mph. A quarter of an hour of this type of question was followed by what I think was a deliberate trick question to see if I had any "Bolshie" attitude.

"Do you ride"? was the question from a Captain. "Equestrian, no Sir, but I do ride a bicycle and there are similarities" I said. "I am surprised that you passed your eyesight medical if you see similarities between the backside of a horse and the back wheel of a bicycle. Explain yourself!" So I explained the need for care in attending to the mechanical needs and welfare of both steeds, the love of countryside aroused in exercising them, the companionship experienced in sharing the hobby with someone of similar interest, and the self-discipline engendered by giving priority to the steed's necessities before one's own.

"I shall look at bicycles in a new light!" said my questioner. There was then a concerted attempt to persuade me to change my application from pilot to observer but I had no doubts in my mind about my choice. After a two minute recess I was called back into the interview room to be told that I was accepted for pilot training in the Fleet Air Arm and would be required to present myself at H.M.S. Daedalus at Lee-on-the-Solent in about three months' time.

It was to be one year and three months later, on October 5th 1942 before this came about, because of ICI's repeated applications for deferment of call-up on the grounds that I was engaged in research of national importance to the war effort. God help any company, which depends upon an 18 year old to such an extent. I reckon that it shows how the self-aggrandisement of an individual such as my Manager can have an adverse effect on his subordinates. I was even prevented from attending a two-week summer camp at the Royal Naval College at Dartmouth on the grounds that it would interfere with progress on the research project on which I was working. That I was offering to forego the whole of my two-week annual leave was deemed irrelevant on the grounds that my work would suffer unless I took the holiday. During that extra year in industry I tried hard not to drop my standards in work, in the Home Guard, and at night school but my weariness took its toll. I tried to keep fit by cross-country running in my half-hour lunch break, and eating my sandwiches between tasks at the laboratory bench. My heart was no longer in the absorption at night school of Pure and Applied Maths, Physics and Chemistry. I concentrated on transmitting and receiving Morse code up to twelve words per minute, together with mastering dead reckoning navigation from a book in the Library. I found myself longing for my call-up day with a passion equal to that of a Dutchman longing for the liberation of his homeland.

Stan Brand as "Old Bill". So our homes are really guarded?

My friends at the laboratory took me out for the night on the eve of my departure, starting off in a public house at one end of Stockton High Street, with the intention of drinking half a pint of beer in every pub, going up one side of the street and down the other. In total there must be at least thirty pubs in the main street of this ancient market town and I was quite incapable of staying the course, ending by being dependent upon my chums to get me home. My parents were very understanding about the condition I was in, which taught me a lesson for the future.

Next day I used the travel warrant provided by the Admiralty for Lee-on-the-Solent to go via Lewes in Sussex in order to visit my grandmother who lived near Cooksbridge, with the added incentive that my cousin John Hopkins (whom I had never met) from Alberta in Canada, would be there, spending a weekend leave from the Canadian Army. I blotted my reputation by being violently sick after what reputedly was a greedy surfeit of unaccustomed fruit from granny's orchard, but which in truth was the alcoholic residue of my colleagues' farewell with a moderate topping of plums and green apples.

Chapter Five

Stone Frigates

I arrived at H.M.S. Daedalus, the Fleet Air Arm station and airfield at Lee-on-the-Solent at about seven pm one Sunday evening, and was handed over to the tender care of a "Stripey", a matelot who had never earned any, (or had forfeited all), promotion in his long years of service but knew all the rules, regulations and dodges. I was issued with blankets, corned beef sandwiches and cocoa and given a place on an iron-framed one-up-one-down bed in a Nissen hut. The hut lacked any heating but had an ablution trough with cold running water and lavatories without any seats or doors. Having just achieved manhood I stoically refrained from crying myself to sleep. After a night disturbed by the resonant snores of my fellow detainees, shivering spells, which caused me to rouse and put on some clothing, there was an unbelievable racket caused by some maniac playing a bugle at the unearthly hour of 6 am. This was the first of many such occasions and was known as "Wakey Wakey" accompanied by unrepeatable words set to the tune by generations of disturbed sailors. After dashing to use the very public toilets, came the indescribable pleasure of queuing for one of the ten places at the one trough available for forty people, splashing and shaving in cold water. We soon learned that safety razor blades never appeared above the counter in the NAAFI, and that cold water shaving blunted a blade in three days, yet we had to be clean-shaven at all times. We learned how to revive a blade by working it back and forth on the inside of a glass tumbler, but the more adventurous amongst us prevailed upon our parents to provide us with the family heirloom; a cut-throat razor and strop. I used one for years but always shaved in the evenings so that I wouldn't get my elbow joggled in the morning scrimmage but I was of very fair complexion and had a soft beard, which didn't intrude upon morning parades.

I must come back to that first day in the Navy. Without a tape-measure appearing once, we were kitted out with every size judged by eye, of which there were numerous inexperienced ones.

51

With armfuls of kit we had to be shown the secrets and intricacies of how to get into, and how to get out of Nelson's square rig matelot's uniform. To get a too-small jumper seized-up over one's head, trapping one's arms in an unusable position was very claustrophobic and cries for help were very muffled. Bell-bottomed trousers had to be tight-fitting anyway, to show off Jack Tar's physique to the best advantage, but, if one got them too small, then the peculiar configuration of the two side crossover flaps and the single vertical flap inflicted such pain that a cry for help was at such a high pitch of urgency that your new-found "oppos" gave immediate assistance. The fit of the sailor headgear is of paramount importance. To convey an Officer-like quality the cap must lie horizontally above both eyes and be tightly secure against wind and weather. For a "Jack-the-Lad" feeling to impress the girls, it must lie flat-a-back precariously poised on the back of the head with no visible means of support, yet remain there during struggles to get to the front of the bar or even during a fracas with "Pongos", (meaning all males wearing a khaki uniform).

Once satisfied with fitting, all gear had to be marked with the owner's name by means of wooden letters clipped together and "inked" with white paint absorbed into a felt pad, so that proof of ownership could never be in doubt. The quality of items issued was very high and the clothes brush (vital with navy-blue serge) and the two shoe brushes (one to apply and the other to polish) are still in daily use nearly sixty years later!

Stripey, the fount of all knowledge, showed us how to lay out our kit for inspection, with a place for everything and everything in its place. We soon learnt that it was essential to be methodical when living communally in restricted space, also that complete honesty was of paramount importance for the peace of mind of everyone and the essential basis for morale and esprit de corps.

Discipline was rigorous and petty officers were on the lookout for sloppy behaviour and noted it against the name of the offender. Ability to handle responsibility was assessed by putting individuals in charge of minor squads on every possible occasion, even when just going from one classroom to another. Parade ground (correction: Quarterdeck) marching and drill had to be impeccable because, as our Petty Officer stressed, you never know when you will have to bury the King or some foreign president at 24 hours' notice. When my turn came to command a squad for drill I had them proceeding at the double down the centre of the quarterdeck, towards the Commodore's bungalow, when the resident Squadron of Avenger torpedo-bomber-reconnaissance aircraft commenced a practice deck-sequence take-off, one after the other, at full throttle, from the adjacent airfield, right over my squad. My power of command paled into insignificance when faced with competition like this, and my delighted squad trotted straight ahead in the absence of any audible command to the contrary, over the well-tended garden in front of the bungalow, up to the window of the Commodore's drawing room which interrupted their progress but allowed them to mark time, at double pace, in the precious border which was the pride and joy of Mrs. Commodore. As the last rasping engine noise went off over the Solent I regained some little control over my fellow Cadets, got them to about-turn and double round and round the Quarterdeck until their hilarity died down. The Chief Petty Officer in charge called me into his office and asked me what I intended to do about the incident.

"Grovel to the Commodore and detail a working party to rectify the damage," I said.

"How will you pick your working party?" asked the C.P.O.

"The chaps with muddy boots," was my reply. Chiefy then told me he would endorse my record with OLQ (officer-like quality)!

Much of our time was occupied with the absorption of Naval tradition and lore but first the Navy saw its prime duty "in loco parentis" was to warn raw recruits of the dangers of consorting with low women and, to that end, had prepared a film in gaudy early Technicolour showing the worst horrors of Venereal Disease in all its stages. In general, we were a pretty innocent bunch of young men from rather sheltered backgrounds who naively connected transmission of such diseases with lavatory seats, and the reality of this presentation left us sick, disillusioned, horrified and alarmed enough to vow to ourselves that we would never expose ourselves to such risks. This also confirmed the principles inculcated at home that any girl fit to be considered as a possible lifelong partner would have to be an undoubted virgin and therefore, as a matter of common decency, one also must remain a "bull virgin".

Other films, pandering to our patriotic fervour, were shown including *Find, Fix and Strike*, *Ships with Wings*, and *In Which We Serve,* all of which helped to dilute the rigours of the basic training which filled the rest of our duty hours.

These were governed by the Naval watch-system giving us alternate evenings off duty when we could attend to our new-fangled uniform and inflict improvements upon it such as scrubbing the blue collar to make it fade to a mature pastel blue from the original navy blue to give the false impression of many washes in long service, coupled with sun-fading on tropical commissions. It was also essential to turn bell-bottomed trousers inside out and crease them in seven concertina folds (representing seven seas) to show that they had spent some considerable time in the confines of a "deep-sea" kitbag. Another time-consuming job was to bring the Navy-issue boots into a light-reflecting state of polish, achieved by liberal application of polish anointed with spit, smoothed in with the back of a spoon warmed in the flame of a candle. All this nonsense was justified, because this is the way it has been done since Nelson (of immortal memory) was a nipper.

When off-duty we were allowed to "go ashore" into the outside world by "getting fell-in" to board an imaginary Liberty Boat, which was launched at half-hourly intervals after rigorous inspection of prospective occupants and woe betide any matelot failing to meet the standards set by the Regulating Petty Officer. The worst possible crime was to attempt to smuggle ashore duty-free tobacco or cigarettes thus jeopardising the privilege of duty-free in shore bases of which the Army and Air Force were justifiably jealous.

As Naval Airmen Second Class (NAII) we were the lowest of the low and were expected to be seasick on the Gosport Ferry. We were paid two shillings (10p) per day, which was handed over once every fourteen days, as accumulated wealth, in an elaborate ritual where we paraded en masse. We waited until our names were called, whereupon one had to double up to a trestle table behind which a junior officer of the Paymaster Branch was sitting. At attention, on the command "Off Cap" we reached with our right hand round to the left hand perimeter of the cap, lifted it off the head and put it down in front of the paymaster. Then with the left hand we placed our pay book, open at the correct page, on top of the cap and the Paymaster would dole out a one-pound note and four two-shilling pieces on to the open pay book. Picking up the pay book and folding it with the left hand so as to trap the note and coins, then with the right hand replacing the cap squarely on the head, executing a smart about turn without scattering the ill-gotten gains to the four winds, was a very elaborate procedure for such a small reward. However it was all part of conditioning us to be thankful for whatever their Lordships of the Admiralty condescended to bestow upon us, even though we had to earn it first.

After four weeks at Daedalus we packed our deep-sea kitbags in the approved fashion and were bussed to HMS St.Vincent, a "stone frigate" which had been a boy-seaman's training unit, at Gosport. The austere appearance coupled with the shouted commands of Petty Officers led one of our wags to assume that we had arrived at the Napoleonic War equivalent of Colditz, the German prisoner-of-war detention centre for persistent escapees. It was only after taking up residence that we realised that the wag's assumption was true and it was no joke. The usual Naval formalities had to be performed to allocate us to Divisions, Watches and Messes and I found myself on duty watch and detailed for fire watching that night. After being issued with blankets I managed to secure a top bunk near to a window in a huge dormitory before going down to the mess where we each collected an individual steak and kidney pie and a dollop of mashed potato with a huge hunk of bread.

The pies had been kept warm on a massive hot plate and a noisy disturbance broke out amongst the first arrivals as they cut open the pies. Swarms of cockroaches, which had entered the pies through the vent holes in the upper crust in search of food and warmth, scurried away under the horrified gaze of the men with the knives. That is, all but the bugs which fell victim to the cut, whose dissected bodies gave out a revolting smell never to be forgotten. The "gash-bins" were hardly big enough to contain so many plate scrapings, and must have brought joy to the heart and pocket of the pig-swill man.

The Duty Officer was called and he made arrangements for the issue of bread, margarine and jam but few of us had any appetite left. Those who had used their cutlery and "blooded" it felt it could never be cleansed properly in the greasy luke-warm water provided for washing. Those of us with a keen sense of smell realised that the mess deck had a most peculiar odour over and above that of rancid fat, socks and underclothing. I later detected this to be the ubiquitous presence of cockroaches. There was a roaring trade in the N.A.A.F.I. canteen that night but our spirits were further dampened when recounting our tale of horror to a member of the senior course ahead of us, who laughed uproariously saying "That's nothing. One of our chaps found a mouse's head in one half of a similar pie but only after finishing the other half. Anyway, when you come through the canteen during fire watching at night, mind you don't get knocked down by herds of scurrying cockroaches when you put the light on". We all developed that lean and hungry look beloved by the Romans and became very trim and very fit at St.Vincent.

Fire watching at St.Vincent was no sinecure in those days of late 1942. Portsmouth and Gosport were the target for frequent raids by the Luftwaffe, starting with incendiary bombs to create fires which acted as markers for the second wave of attackers with high explosive bombs. The incendiaries also brought Air Raid Precaution

(ARP) Wardens, Firemen and NAIIs out of their shelters, and exposed them to the high explosives which reduced the numbers of trained and experienced personnel available to defend against subsequent attacks. Our equipment consisted of long handled (6 feet) shovels and rakes and buckets of sand to smother magnesium-based igniters by depriving them of the air necessary for combustion, and "stirrup pumps" which were hand operated pumps designed for the peaceful watering of garden patches. The water supply for these had to be carried in a bucket to a position within four yards of the fire because of the limited range of the jet of water produced. Since incendiary bombs usually came to rest in roof gutters or loft spaces with difficult access, getting fire-fighting equipment to the point of application, in the blackout, in strange territory, with bombs falling, was no task for the fainthearted. But it had to be done, done quickly, and by the people nearest to hand. In the absence of an air raid warning we could sleep, but some nights left us boggle-eyed and ready to doze off in lectures, a heinous offence and without doubt an un-officer-like quality.

One Sunday morning after Divisions, (the open-air service held on the quarterdeck), I went to my bunk to do some swotting and I heard the Royal Marines Band strike up a rousing "Hearts of Oak" march on the vacated quarterdeck. Hoping to get a grandstand view I stood on the bottom bunk and bridged the gap between it and the high window ledge by falling forward and putting my hand out to rest on the window ledge.

I hadn't seen that someone had parked a threaded needle by sticking the point into the wood, and the eye went through the palm of my hand ending up sticking up through the back of my hand, needle and thread passing through the hand and the needle point with a foot or so of thread sticking through the palm. Doubting the sterility of the needle and thread, which could have been gathering dust and germs for months out of sight up there, I felt it wise to go to Sick Bay to remove the offending foreign bodies. At the double, for all movement had to be at this speed, I skirted the quarterdeck and in spite of my haste I noticed something familiar about an NAII doubling towards me. It was my second cousin, Frank Dane!

Neither of us had been aware of the other's intention to join the Fleet Air Arm, which perhaps was not surprising as we met only once each year during family visits to my grandmother. Frank was on the 45th Pilots' Course, following my 44th but four weeks later.

I about-turned and made myself known then excused myself by displaying my predicament and went on to the Sick Bay for the necessary attention after which I sought out Frank again. It was the beginning of one year of close friendship, which was disrupted by Frank's decision to train as a fighter pilot and mine to go for torpedo-bomber-reconnaissance training, and terminating with Frank's death in his Seafire in the Pacific in 1945 close to the end of the war with Japan. We shared many happy experiences during our time at Elementary Flying Training and Service Flying Training Schools, both on course and off duty, at Sealand in Cheshire and in Kingston, Ontario.

The course at St.Vincent was a horror as far as food and accommodation were concerned but I found the subject matter of lectures to be extremely interesting and very well put over by experienced Petty Officers and young Lieutenants. We had little time for anything but navigation by dead reckoning, seamanship, reading charts and maps, signalling by flags, semaphore, Aldis lamp, and wireless, how to tie knots and where to use the variants, rules of the road at sea, ships' lights and their meanings, recognition of the different kinds of buoys and their purpose, small arms and ammunition, naval tradition and customs, ship and aircraft recognition at the subliminal speed of one twenty-fifth of a second, and so on. Interspersed with "square-bashing", physical training and passing the Navy's swimming survival test, the eight-week course flew past and the examinations were upon us. There was a failure rate of about 25% and we survivors were promoted to Leading Naval Airmen and sewed an anchor badge on our left sleeves. This ranked senior to a corporal in the other services and rightly so in view of the standard of examination, but we were later to find that few members of the RAF were aware of this, and confusedly equated Leading Naval Airman with Leading Aircraftsman who was only on a level with an Able Seaman. It is remarkable how frequently the seniority was claimed when privileges were in question and kept quiet when blame or duty was to be allocated. Was this a display of officer-like qualities?

Leading Naval Airman, Stanley Brand, in December 1942. Rating known as a "Killick" (naval slang for an anchor).

The course came to an end at Christmas 1942 and we were sent on leave for a fortnight. The whole nation had hoped that one Christmas after another would have seen the end of the war and this was no exception. Even so, there were very few signs of despondency in spite of a surfeit of disasters and a shortage of successes. Whether this was due to a bloody-minded refusal to face up to facts, or a heroic and indomitable spirit has been the subject of much subsequent debate.

As one who was there, I am certain that it was a combination of both. In fact the spirit gave rise to the inability to accept defeat. We didn't know when we were beaten. The possibility was quite unacceptable, so we collected together what treats we could from our meagre rations, toasted our many absent friends with some revolting home brews and "made the best of a bad job". Some of us went to Church to plead for the safe return of missing and absent loved ones and to pray for some news even if it had to be from a prisoner-of-war camp. Then, thankful for very small mercies we got on with our lives.

Chapter Six

Airborne At Last!

Soon it was time for half of No.44 Pilots' Training Course to go to the next stage of their training at Elmdon Aerodrome (after the war this became Birmingham Airport) whilst the other half, myself included, went to No.24 Elementary Flying Training School at Sealand near Chester. The latter was built as an RAF Training School in the late 1930s and was a typical example of the difference in attitude between Lord Trenchard and Lord Nelson towards their troops. In the ablutions there was constant hot water even at the time of greatest demand after a cross-country run which finished immediately before we came "off duty" and could go out of camp. No liberty-boats here. There were even hand basins -with plugs! Toilets -with doors! A cafeteria, with second helpings on request! Beds -with sheets, pillows and pillowcases! So this was how the "Brylcreem boys" (so-called because of liberal application of their favourite hair cream which enabled them to keep their immaculate coiffure in place even in the slipstream of a Spitfire) interpreted the Latin word "ardua"(hardship) in their motto "Per ardua ad astra". We translated this as "Through hardships to the stars". They had no idea what hardships were!

Our Senior Naval Officer at Sealand was Lieutenant Commander Hawkins R.N., a man who we came to respect and to some degree, worship. He was firm, fair, positive and decisive, and had been wounded in action. Grounded, he aimed to pass on to his charges the skills necessary for a Fleet Air Arm pilot to succeed and survive. Of such a man, so much was expected and so much given, and on such men the Service depended. He was the object of the hero-worship of many in the courses which passed through his charge, and it is my fervent wish that youngsters of today could find stars as worthy of admiration as Hawkins was of ours, instead of lavishing their adoration on screeching, moaning, unwashed, unshaven, hip-undulating, drug abusing, sexually promiscuous

61

guttersnipes who never earned the ridiculous fortunes so willingly provided by their witless devotees. This is an ancient generation speaking, as of right, because of our contribution to society and the principles to which we subscribe. Bloody old dinosaurs!

Once again the course was divided into two halves; one to fly whilst the other attended lectures, morning and afternoon turns about. Each half was now down to about thirty men and these were further divided into five flights of six. Thirty was an ideal number for lectures, which were given in huts in the hangar area. Each flight had three instructors and three Tiger Moth aircraft and was allocated a Nissen hut on the airfield perimeter track. Here we became very excited and stimulated by trying on our newly issued flying kit, and absorbing the contents of the "Pilot's Notes" for the DH82a Tiger Moth. We climbed over and sat in our own "tiggy" until we were familiar with all the instruments, controls, knobs, switches, buttons and levers. In those days very few people of our age and social strata had the opportunity to learn to drive, so we were not familiar with the learning process, which would stand today's youth in good stead.

In good flying weather, a pupil could theoretically get two hours' flying in a morning session while his colleague with the same instructor would only get one hour in the afternoon because of daylight limitations in midwinter months. The dominating factor was, of course, the weather, and in my experience this restricted flying in January to seven hours and fifteen minutes in the eight days on which it was fit to fly.

My first flight came six days after my arrival at Sealand, held up for three days by sleet, snow, rain then overcast sky with poor visibility. Those days were not wasted, as they were a great opportunity to absorb the huge amount of information available in our new surroundings. My instructor, Sergeant Pilot Watt, and I had already gone through the petrol, oil, ignition and lubrication system of the Tiger Moth, and I had been taught the airscrew hand-swinging method and procedure of starting-up the engine. The aerodrome layout and circuit procedure had been explained and absorbed, areas to be avoided impressed upon my mind, and areas where low flying was permitted noted with anticipation. I had to sign a statement in my virgin flying logbook to the effect that I fully understood all such matters. My parachute was donned and the straps adjusted to prevent my emasculation in the event of bailing out, and helmet and goggles fitted to stop draughts which would make my eyes water. At last I was seated and strapped in and my means of communication plugged in. The latter consisted of pieces of small-bore rubber tubing connecting the earpieces and speaking funnels of pupil and instructor, down which one had to shout with so much effort that the message was so distorted that it could be understood, if ever, only on the third or fourth attempt. I suppose it was marginally faster than writing and passing notes to each other, and it was amazing how accurately the verbal message could be conveyed in the event of dire emergency, such as "abandon your attempt to land because there is another plane fifty feet below us", normally communicated as "LOOK OUT! I'VE GOT HER! ARE YOU BLIND, YOU STUPID BUGGER?

The engine was started up via the following routine. "Switches off, petrol on, throttle closed, suck in", whereupon the ground crewman turned the propeller by hand for two revolutions to fill the engine cylinders with a mixture of air and petrol vapour. Then "Contact", whereupon the pilot switched on the electrical magneto which would provide the ignition spark, and the ground crewman, holding the very tip of the propeller swung it with force enough to turn the engine, compress the charge in the cylinders and produce the spark which ignited the charge and sprung the engine into life. Or so we hoped. In that winter of 1942/3, with twenty-year-old Tiger Moths picketed out in the open and unsheltered airfield, used by inexperienced pupil pilots and maintained by inexperienced or second line mechanics, readiness to leap into life on a cold morning was not the most prominent attribute of these remarkable old warhorses. In fact, once they were started, they were stopped only for refuelling and were left ticking over whilst instructors and pupils were changed. On this occasion, my first ever flight, we had so many attempts to start, without success, that it was necessary to switch off the ignition and petrol and turn the engine to blow out the excess of petrol which had accumulated during our efforts before recommencing the routine starting procedure. It was a lesson, which I was to use frequently on subsequent dark mornings of that bitterly cold winter.

At last she was coaxed into life and Sgt. Watt went through the warm up and run up procedure before waving the chocks away from our wheels so we could trundle away to our take-off point downwind. Without brakes, one had to keep speed down and steer a zigzag course in order to see straight ahead beyond the obscuring nose of the plane in order to stop before hitting an obstruction such as another aircraft.

A fast revving propeller acts like a huge bacon slicer and makes short work of a "tiggy". Sgt. Watt kept up a running commentary the whole time so that I knew just why he was making every move. As it was a grass field with only one runway (which was out of bounds to pupils), we taxied to the downwind boundary and turned crosswind so that we had a clear view of any aircraft coming in to land. There was no control van or system at Sealand and it was the pilots' responsibility to ensure there was no interference with incoming aircraft. As soon as it was safe Sgt. Watt turned into wind, opened the throttle and launched me into the job I had wanted to do ever since I had watched Alan (later Sir Alan) Cobham's Flying Circus operate from a field near my home, eating my heart out because I hadn't the five shillings which was the price of a flip in his first-world-war-surplus Avro 504.

We rumbled and jolted across the grass field as we gathered speed and our tail came up off the ground and then came the wonderful transformation as we became airborne.

As a chrysalis releases the bonds holding back the newborn butterfly from its true destiny, so we were transformed from being a clumsy, labouring, roaring, bouncing contraption as we left earth behind and became a soaring, purring, smooth, unfettered entity with the world at our feet. No wonder that philosophers through the ages have always associated their ideas of Heaven with the provision of wings together with the concept of Heaven being way up there above the clouds. Although Sgt. Watts had been telling me of his every action and the reason for it and I had mentally recorded his every word, I was so filled with wonder and excitement that I was entranced until he brought me down to earth again. My logbook records tersely "Air Experience 20 mins". I was dropped back at the Flight crew-hut and my opposite number went off to experience his first taste of flight, and the air sickness which was to end his air training after persistent attempts to accustom him to the motion of flying, and to overcome his problem, without success. In mid-January he was summoned to the SNO's office out of a lecture and that was the last we saw of him. No goodbyes, no opportunity to exchange contact addresses or to commiserate, just an empty bed and locker in our dormitory. This approach to parting of the ways was, perhaps, one way of preparing us for the inevitable casualties we were to experience in the future. The main difference, we were to learn the hard way was when we had to sort out the personal effects of a casualty, whereas a failed pilot sorted out and packed his own kit.

With the initial weeding out of pupils totally unsuited for flying training, more instructor time and Tiger Moth time was released, to the great advantage of survivors who were then able to get closer to their instructor and also benefit from the greater availability of a plane when a break in the poor weather occurred. Reduction in the number remaining on the course also presented opportunities for instructors to take up their quota of leave, though it was rumoured that some instructors would create a spate of failures amongst their pupils in order to create a suitable gap around a preferred date for taking their leave. I am quite sure that this view was libellous, because an independent check was always made by another instructor, who gave the benefit of any doubt to the pupil. It was true that an instructor who accumulated an unusually high number of failures of his students to his discredit could then devote all of his attention to his remaining pupils who then had a better chance of success than they would have had otherwise.

To hear one's instructor say for the first time " You've got her" as he handed over the controls, gave a surge of adrenaline as one took over the joystick, rudder bar and throttle. Flying straight and level, climbing and descending, all had to be mastered with a gentle touch and sensitive correction. A tendency to grip the controls had to be consciously overcome and replaced with a light thumb-and-forefinger hold, through which one could feel what messages the ailerons and elevators sent back through their connecting wires. Gentle turns without gaining or losing height followed, then came climbing and descending turns, with and without power from the engine. Repetition and more repetition let instinct take charge and at this stage more adventurous manoeuvres were introduced, the most exhilarating being landing and takeoff. As soon as the pupil showed competence without overconfidence he was nearing his first solo flight and therefore had to be introduced to the hazard of spinning, which he could meet by failing to maintain his airspeed whilst concentrating on something else. The way into a spin and quick recovery out of it had to be practised until it was instinctive not to get into one and alternatively to get out of one speedily whilst there was still enough height to do so.

After seven hours and fifty-five minutes of dual instruction in the Tiger Moth, I was given a solo test, by a Flight Lieutenant from another Flight. It lasted a full hour and covered everything I had been taught so far, and simulated every emergency that might occur. I landed the plane and taxied in to the crew hut dispersal and was very relieved when my examiner told me to stay where I was while he climbed out of the front seat and secured his unfastened safety harness to prevent it from interfering with the flying controls.

Then he clapped me on the shoulder and said, "She's all yours. Take her once round the circuit and don't forget there are others around you. If you don't like the situation, go round again. Best of luck, though you don't need it."

So off I went. After taxiing to the downwind end of the grass field, which was Sealand, I turned crosswind so that I could see all incoming aircraft and then I did the pre-flight check. There seemed to be a never-ending stream of traffic and I had to restrain myself from trying to squeeze in, in case my Instructor who would be watching might think that I was a frightened chicken. At last the timing was right and I turned into wind and opened up the throttle. Up came the tail and we (Tiggy and I) gathered speed rapidly, feeling so buoyant without the weight of the instructor in the front seat, and with every bump in the grass threatening to get us airborne before we were quite ready. Suddenly there was a beautiful smoothness as we were supported by the wonders of aerodynamics. The blur of grass stems raced past and then as my chariot bore me into Wonderland, I climbed up into my new domain at the prescribed airspeed, throttled back the engine and leaned-out the mixture. I was too busy to look down at the crew-hut to see how many admirers were watching me. At eight hundred feet I had to do a climbing turn on to the upwind cross leg of the circuit watching out all the time for any aircraft joining the circuit, which could have an instructor in it capable of giving an adverse report on my lookout awareness. Levelling out at one thousand feet, throttling back to prevent an increase in speed, then turning left (not "to port", for I was still with the RAF) on to the downwind leg of the circuit kept me busy for a while, but then I had to check the "T" (which indicated the landing direction in the Control Tower information square) to make sure that the landing direction had not been changed whilst I was airborne.

This had to happen sometime, and God help the pupil who added to the inevitable confusion by failing to notice the change and flying in at ninety degrees to everyone else, especially on his first solo flight.

The "T" was still pointing in the same direction as when I took off, so I continued on the downwind leg until the landing point was at one hundred and twenty degrees on the left of my line of flight. I then turned left, crosswind, and throttled back completely to do a glide approach, having made sure during the turn that there was no other aircraft beneath me on the approach to land. With the engine ticking over and gently losing height I was soon down to six hundred feet and ready to turn on to the final approach. Now fully committed, I realised that I was rather too high and would touch down well into the field, so I side-slipped some height away until I came over the boundary fence at about fifty feet, brought the stick back slowly and gently until I lost flying speed and could see the grass-stems individually just below my wing. With a gentle rumble I WAS DOWN!

I taxied in to dispersal and after blipping the engine just to let everyone know I was back (though they had all been standing outside the crew hut so as not to miss any excitement), I cut the ignition. As nonchalantly as possible undid my straps, opened up the half-door and climbed out trying to hide the knee-tremble which I was sure must be obvious to everyone. My instructor met me to ask why didn't I always make a landing like that! The old saying "He was like a dog with two tails" should be replaced by "He was like a sprog pilot who had just gone solo". It was hard not to commiserate with course-mates who were nearing the twelve hours of dual instruction, which set the alarm bells of possible failure ringing in the office of the Chief Flying Instructor, who would then institute his personal test.

To deflate the ego of the new soloist, came instrument flying on the first subsequent flight. Under a canvas hood and by the light of luminous instruments which could be seen only with difficulty came half-hour sessions of straight and level flight progressing through level turns to climbing and descending turns and then to turns on to compass courses. It was seven hours and twenty-five minutes of dual instruction and three weeks later before I was free to fly solo again, because of appalling weather in that February of 1943 and a vicious attack of tonsillitis, which dropped me back from the 44th to the 45th Pilot's Course. When fully recovered and a break in the weather finally came I had five flights in one day, two of them solo but all confined to take-off and landings on the circuit because the visibility was so bad. Over the next few days, as the visibility progressively improved my instructor took me away from the circuit to do instrument flying, spinning, and forced landings when he would cut the engine without warning. From that time onwards I would always select the best landing space within gliding distance and keep it in mind until it was out of range, by which time I would have picked the next possibility. This training stood me in good stead right through my flying career, especially in 1996 whilst flying Microlite aircraft when I had three engine failures in twenty-five hours of flying but got down safely without any damage and was able to fly out again after repair.

Next came a triangular cross-country flight with my instructor riding "shotgun" to take action only if I got into difficulties. Fortunately, maps had always held a fascination for me and this exercise presented no difficulties. From then onwards I was allowed off the circuit for all appropriate exercises. With twenty-eight hours of dual instruction and fourteen hours solo I graduated to triangular cross-country flights on my own together with solo spinning, forced landings (which provided an excuse for illicit low flying), and aerobatics.

The latter were restricted to spinning, steep and stall turns and looping the loop until I had thirty-three hours of dual and I was then introduced to slow rolls dual before gaining permission to do them solo.

My elementary flying training drew to a close with three hours of night flying and a Chief Flying Instructor's Test, certifying me as "fit for solo at night but weather conditions unfit". So, after thirty-six hours and five minutes dual by day including eight hours and fifty minutes of instrument flying, together with twenty-five hours and thirty minutes solo by day and three hours dual by night, my elementary flying training was complete. I was now ready to continue with Service Flying Training at No. 31 S.F.T.S. at Kingston Ontario, Canada, under the Empire Air Training Scheme.

Early in the War it was found that Jerry located flying training airfields in the U.K. and was able to shoot down trainer aircraft, with their valuable instructors and carefully selected trainees with little or no danger to themselves. An additional advantage in sending trainees to either Canada or South Africa was the reliability of weather, which gave the continuity of instruction, which is so important to a pupil pilot who needs to practise what he has been taught without delay if it is to be absorbed.

----ooOoo----

De Havilland Tiger Moth DH82a
The beloved "Tiggy"

Chapter Seven

Cunard Cruise and Cook's Tour

The journey from Sealand to Kingston was a long and circuitous route. Ten days of leave at home confirmed that my engagement to a girl called Betty, whom I had met at ICI in 1940, was over because she had met, and become attached to, an invalided repatriated soldier who had been a prisoner-of-war of the Germans. From home I went back to Lee-on-the-Solent and thence to a boarding house in Blackpool. Here we were paraded three times a day, for several weeks, to make sure that we had not deserted. At very short notice we then boarded a troop train, (without corridor or toilet facilities), for a fifteen-hour journey to Gourock on the Clyde, where at 3am. we were given a beans and bacon breakfast (without eating irons) from an Army field-kitchen in a draughty dockside warehouse (without seating). It was rumoured that we would be expected to board our troopship now at anchor at the Tail o' the Bank, off Greenock (without the use of a tender), but fortunately for us one of the Transport Officer's staff had made the mistake of organising a Clyde ferry which arrived at 2 pm. and took us out to the magnificent *Queen Elizabeth* which towered above us and, unbelievably, seemed to be expecting us. From the moment we clambered aboard, our fortunes changed. We were escorted to outer cabins on the upper deck, where we were allocated six to a double luxury cabin with en-suite bathroom and toilet. It had been fitted with six folding-down pipe-framed beds in place of the intended double bed, and all six were made up with sheets, blankets and pillows with pillowcases! We stowed our gear in mahogany-lined wardrobes and drawers and shuddered at the desecration "Kilroy was here" scrawled in the most obvious places alongside the initials, hometown and dates of the last U.S. Midwestern occupants. I hoped they had been desperately seasick, but over the side, not inboard.

Half an hour after boarding there was a pipe "All passengers who arrived after 1200hrs. are to go to the dining room on No. 2

deck where a late lunch will be served". Arriving there sedately although a little out-of-breath, because it would have been sacrilege to go there at the double in such a cathedral, we were astounded to see white damask tablecloths on which reposed dishes of butter, platters of white bread, and most surprising of all, knives, forks and spoons all laid out at about thirty inch spacing. Incongruously, there was no waiter service. We actually had to queue-up for a tray and self-service soup and main course and pudding. I was so overwhelmed that some detail didn't register. I do recall, however, the huge block of orange-coloured American cheese on the table to go with the crusty, freshly baked virginally white bread and corn-yellow butter with a real butter flavour without even the slightest hint of axle grease. It fulfilled the dreams of a healthy nineteen-year-old who had just survived into his fourth year of rationing. By five o'clock I was fast asleep on my bunk and at six o'clock wide-awake wondering what delights Cunard had in store for the evening meal. We were not disappointed, then or at any time in the next four days. There was also a shop, which sold unlimited (except by money) Hershey chocolate bars, which we grudgingly accepted even though they didn't taste quite right compared to our fond memory of Cadbury flavour. For some odd reason that we didn't understand, the dining room queues shortened distinctly from the time our lovely ship upped anchor and headed out across the Atlantic. Squirrel instinct showed in our acquisition of razor blades, toilet soap and cigarettes but we were soon parted from our small store of sterling left after those purchases by the wise guys who knew the finer points of the three card trick and the game Crown and Anchor.

My cousin Frank and I joined the queue of those millions of penniless, destitute immigrants who watched the welcoming torch of the Statue of Liberty as we sailed into New York Harbour (with apologies- Harbor) only four days after leaving the Clyde.

It was rumoured that there would be a long delay in docking because of a strike by the Longshoremen, Tugboatmen and Dockers Union but this did not come about because the Captain decided to go in without their assistance, probably commenting "Don't you know there's a war on?" Proudly the 80,000 ton ship moved in serenely like the Queen she was and took up her rightful position by the Pier, kissing it gently before taking her repose after a tiring journey. For some reason we felt even more proud of the uniform we were wearing as we "got fell in" on the quayside to be "bussed" to the Grand Union Station where we were put on a special train along with about three hundred RAF types heading for a posting station at Moncton, New Brunswick.

It took nearly thirty hours to reach Moncton, sustained by packed meals and a special stop organised by the Canadian Army testing its ability to feed an army on the move with a field kitchen which provided a beef stew followed by a huge Sirloin steak with lashings of what we would come to know as French Fries, but were happy to accept as "chips", with fried tomatoes, bigger than we had ever seen, together with deep fried battered onion rings, which we had never seen before. Ice cream of any mixture of about ten flavours including many unknown and unheard-of, rounded off this feast, introducing us to the wartime hardships and the unbounded generosity of North America. Expecting Moncton to expose us to the pioneer standards we must meet sooner or later, we were thrilled to find centrally heated blocks, held at a temperature of about 72 degrees Fahrenheit and with constant scalding-hot water fed by culverted steam pipes which kept footpaths clear of snow. After our long journey we were desperate to soak in the luxurious baths and then get our heads down for uninterrupted sleep, between crisply laundered sheets provided by the Royal Canadian Air Force.

A week of idleness followed, interrupted only by one parade each day, one of which was a pay parade giving us ten Canadian dollars each, after which we were allowed out into the town. The complete absence of public houses was of no hardship with so many new things and so much affluence around us. The quality and quantity of food in camp made it unnecessary for us to spend on food but nevertheless we explored the novelty of Drug Stores with their multiplicity of "sodas" and milk shakes, hamburgers and hot-dogs. Our teenage frames were lean and fit enough after years of rationing and Naval deprivation to take these excesses in our stride. What we were not prepared for was the readiness, willingness and ability of the local young ladies to enter into a "necking session" with such enthusiasm yet to terminate it adroitly and precisely at the crucial moment when our naivety told us that we were on to a good thing. It appeared that the New World was years ahead of us in this skill as in so many others.

After a week of "lotus-eating" we paraded with all our kit to entrain for our destination at No. 31 Service Flying Training School. This time the train consisted of coaches from the pioneer period after the first World War when ex-servicemen were offered plots of undeveloped land in the wilder parts of Canada in order to open-up the country.

Several of my aunts and uncles, together with my grandmother, participated in this scheme and were taken by train to Peace River in September 1920 where they were left to find their allocated plots many miles out in the scrubland with the autumn nearly over and the rigours of a Canadian winter about to descend upon them. Without time to fell and saw timber to build a cabin, these Flanders veterans made revetted dugouts and went to earth for that first winter, surviving on berries gathered and preserved by the womenfolk and rabbits trapped or shot by the males before the worst of their bitterly cold ordeal hid even firewood from them.

The Spartan conditions of the rail coaches gave us some concept of the pioneer lifestyle. The wooden slatted seats without upholstery soon restricted the circulation in our meagrely padded bums. The overhead drop-down bunks with canvas suspension provided necessary relief but there were not enough of them to go round, so we arranged amongst ourselves a workable rota. The journey from Moncton New Brunswick to Kingston Ontario was over in less than thirty hours compared with the seven days my relatives endured from Halifax in Nova Scotia to Peace River Alberta.

We had a five-hour break in Montreal for sightseeing, which no doubt, was not included in the itinerary of my grandmother. In the Montreal sidings where we were parked we hastily pooled our depleted cash to hire a cab and approached a taxi driver to show us the city as far as twelve dollars would take us. This was on a Sunday morning at about 9 am. and no doubt our conversation somewhere mentioned breakfast so we were not surprised when the driver pulled up outside what appeared to be a bed and breakfast establishment with a veranda and a flight of about five steps up to it. We piled out and just got to the foot of the steps when a Royal Canadian Navy Lieutenant came out of the door and seemed to be a little disconcerted by our presence. Being Officer Cadets and on our best behaviour we gave him gangway and one of our party called us to attention and saluted and he responded in kind but, we thought, rather sloppily and reluctantly, before he moved rapidly through us as if he were running the gauntlet. That over, we went on up the stairs and found the door held open by a motherly looking woman who looked as if she had experienced hard times in her youth, who welcomed us into a sitting room and told us to make ourselves at home while she got things ready for us. We conferred over the state of our assets because we had not envisaged incurring a meal bill and we decided upon offering our apologies and retreating, when there was a gentle rustling of diaphanous feminine clothing and in came six women naked except for some inadequate concealment from which we averted our eyes in embarrassment. They were probably the night shift who would have been on their way home but for our arrival. Just as if we had been pounced upon by a squadron of Me 109s, we simultaneously turned tail and fled, piling into the taxi as if it was a haven to protect us from a fate worse than death. That introductory Technicolor film shown to us at Lee-on-the-Solent had left the scent of fear upon every one of us.

Deprived of his commission, or benefits in kind, our taxi driver was no longer the paternally benign person whom we had engaged earlier that morning and by mutual consent we decided that enough was enough and we wanted to return to the security of our railway carriage, where we were compelled to relate our experience amidst much hilarity and ribaldry to each and every group of our chums as they returned.

Having lost none of our force to the enemy, we re-mustered and continued with our exercise. Admiring the St. Lawrence Seaway and eventually arriving at the shores of Lake Ontario we were fascinated by the beauty of the Thousand Islands dotted around the eastern end of the Lake, and anticipated with some relish the opportunity to fly around them in close-up. We transferred from train to coach at Kingston and rode the six or seven miles out to the airfield. There we were welcomed with a magnificent cafeteria-style meal then shown to our billets before being issued with summer weight Canadian Army-style beige coloured shirts and trousers which were to be our rig-of-the-day for our time at 31 SFTS, with a promise of continuous fine weather and continental temperatures. The airfield bordered upon Lake Ontario with fine beaches, bays and ten-foot cliffs for diving into deep clear water and after our dusty train journey we were soon cavorting about in this wonderful June environment. This was to be our Heaven until the fall, which would arrive in September.

Skylarking in Moncton
Top L to R: Ray Lygo, Stanley Brand
Bottom: Frank Dane, Mike Levitt, Gordon Dunning

Chapter Eight
Canadian Capers

Duty called next morning in the shape of our instructors, who spent a full day with us climbing over Harvard Aircraft parked on tarmac in front of the hangars. They explained all the detail of this, to us, complicated real aeroplane with starter, retractable undercarriage, flaps, brakes, variable pitch propeller, engine boost, etc. The following day we had a blindfold check in the cockpit to ensure that we could put our hands on the appropriate controls and switches and know where to look for gauges to inform us of vital temperatures, pressures and so on. Cockpit checks had to be understood and memorised, and then came the first flight in this powerful, roaring beast which, no doubt, would devour us unless we mastered it at once, and maintained that mastery without one moment's relaxation of control.

The first flight in the Harvard covered a multitude of "firsts". First time in the front seat, first efficient and clear intercommunication, first attempt to cope with a bewildering array of instruments, first hydraulics system, vacuum system, brakes, steerable tailwheel, retractable undercarriage, flaps, propeller pitch control, starter, cockpit heater, radio, gun button, pitot-head heater, landing lights, bomb switches, oil cooler shutter control, gun sight, cine camera, cockpit canopy, etc. Only a Superman can ever cope with it all. So I have to become one. At least there are tarmac or concrete aprons, perimeter tracks and runways everywhere so that there is no danger of getting bogged down as there was at Sealand, or bouncing around on take-off or landing due to hills and valleys rutted into the grass.

Once more the superb quality of instruction was demonstrated in that first familiarisation flight, with a running commentary given by my tutor, so that I missed nothing of importance by preoccupation with the novelties. The most impressive moment was the surge of power on take-off with boosted revs and fine pitch, giving rise to the unmistakable Harvard roar as the propeller tips breached the speed of sound. This was followed by intense activity getting wheels up, throttling back with coarsening pitch, raising flaps, reporting "airborne" to control, and rubbernecking all the time to keep clear of all those other aircraft which kept appearing from nowhere. There was no time at all to appreciate the magnificent view of Lake Ontario, the Thousand Islands, the International Bridge at Watertown and the myriad small lakes which formed half of the landscape under a canopy of impossibly-blue sky seen elsewhere only on unbelievably garish postcards. This was later to become an obsession with me when I had mastered the real purpose of my presence in Canada and had time to enjoy the finer points.

Four weeks of hard graft and concentration followed. At the end of the first week, with eight hours and fifteen minutes of dual instruction achieved in seven half-days of good flying weather, I had an independent check to assess my readiness, and was sent on a forty minute solo flight, and allowed off the circuit. Aerobatics and navigation, map reading and course steering, instrument flying and blind take-offs followed, instilling confidence and producing sheer enjoyment.

Then disaster, in the form of abdominal pains, struck me in the middle of one night as I lay in the bottom bunk under the one occupied by my cousin Frank. I became delirious with a feverish temperature, slipping in and out of sleep, and a short while before "Wakey Wakey", my moans disturbed Frank who woke me up and coerced me to report sick

Suddenly the pains vanished, and I was almost convinced that it had all been a nightmare. I washed, shaved and dressed and went in to breakfast. Over the table Frank told my chums what had happened, and in the discussion which followed one chap told of his brother who had an appendix which ruptured, with serious consequences and he persuaded me to see the Medical Officer. From his examination onwards my feet didn't touch the ground. Within

80

two hours I had been transferred to the Kingston Military Hospital, and because I had taken food I couldn't be given a general anaesthetic, I was injected in the spine with the then almost experimental epidural. Numb from the chest down, I lay on the theatre table and found that I had a first-class view of the proceedings via a multi-mirror reflector around the overhead lights. These were not switched on because they were unnecessary in the brilliant Canadian summer light coming in through the glass dome of the theatre. I watched with great interest as the surgeon made the incision, fished around for the appendix, sutured it off and parted off the offending bit, then started a mopping-up operation. This involved pulling out what they could, wiping and dusting everything with a white powder, which was probably the current wonder cure-all, sulpha-drug. Everything tucked back in, the army surgeon commenced sewing up his handiwork, so with true inter-service cooperation I commented "If you need any advice on knots, you've a naval expert here" which broke the tension accumulated over the previous forty minutes or so. After a few moments the surgeon asked how I knew what stage he was at, and I explained my line of sight, "Cover his eyes at once" he ordered, seeming quite concerned, but without any enthusiasm for Combined Operations.

Next morning the Sister in charge of the ward, Sister Maud McGrath got me up to walk around the ward as was their normal routine after spinal anaesthetic. As it was such a beautiful day, I was wheeled out in a chair and parked in the shade of a huge maple and left to read. After a while some Canadian army Commandos started to throw sticks up into the tree above me. Knowing that they were survivors from the Dieppe Raid and that none came tougher than Canadian Commandos, I decided not to order them to stop larking about, as I felt pretty sure that they would just love to garrotte me before kicking me to death. Then there was a "plop" as a brown paper rugby-football fell out of the tree and landed beside the wheelchair. It emitted a low-pitched, but high volume hum as the squadrons of hornets inside the nest got their order to scramble and intercept the enemy which had the nerve to attack their homeland without prior provocation or good reason. Understandably they transmitted a "Tally- Ho" as soon as they saw me and peeled off into the attack. I girded up my loins, clutched my belly in both arms and high-tailed it for the sanctuary of the ward, which was at least eighty yards away. I am sure I beat the record for a variation on the three-legged race with a comfortable margin to spare. The eighteen confirmed stings, which the hornets managed to inflict, put me on my back and kept me in the ward for three days. The narcotic pain killers which Maudie administered made me dream I was being chased by a pack of wolves and that I kept tripping over my bowels which wouldn't stay inside me and slipped through my fingers, despite feverish attempts to stuff them back. I regretted the bravado that had led me to watch the operation.

Discharged from hospital within a week, I was given three weeks of sick leave, but knew that I could not face the five-day train journey to visit my aunt and cousins in Peace River, Alberta. The Padre suggested that I should go to Chicago where there was an organisation designed specifically for Servicemen in my predicament, and he made arrangements for me to be met off the train in Chicago by Mrs. Bright, a wonderfully motherly person whose three sons were all serving in the American forces. Taken to her home on the south side of Chicago, I was given the bedroom of one of her sons, shown around the house and given the complete freedom of being at home. Although it was early evening I went to bed and slept soundly between lavender-scented crisp sheets, which reminded me of childhood holidays at my grandmother's home in Sussex. Next morning I was awakened with a tray bearing an American breakfast - hickory smoked streaky bacon, two eggs sunny side up, waffles with maple syrup, with toast, butter and marmalade to follow, and a large pot of real American coffee kept hot on an electrically heated plate (which was new to me). No wonder that on completion, I turned over and went back to sleep again until well after mid-day. On my dressing table I found a "bill-fold" wallet in an envelope addressed to me by Mr. Bright, containing American dollars in profusion together with a book of tickets for the "EL", the elevated railway serving the whole of Chicago and its environs. Hospitality such as this was beyond my expectations and I hoped that

American servicemen found a similar welcome in the UK but in reality I know that they didn't.

That afternoon, one of Mrs. Bright's daughters, who was a Doctor of Jurisprudence, drove me into the United Services Organisation (USO) and introduced me to the Committee of Welcome who in turn appointed a matronly lady to be my Helper. She gave me the low-down on all the facilities available to a Services visitor together with leaflets and documents to support my memory, amounting to a carrier bag full of interesting information, in fact, too much to absorb. Over coffee and sandwiches which I chose in preference to the full meal offered, I met a USN Petty Officer, Piet Larsen, who was stationed at The Great Lakes Navy Air Corps Base a few miles North of Chicago. He was very interested in the British way of Naval Aviation and gave me an invitation to visit his station and meet his Commanding Officer. I can hardly imagine the reciprocal occurrence at Lee-on-the-Solent. I took him up on the invitation and a week later made the visit and formed a firm friendship with Piet, which lasted and was reinforced by frequent letters until he went out to the Pacific in 1944 from where I had a letter returned to my home address marked "deceased." I regretted not having established contact with his family. Piet Larsen was of second generation Norwegian stock and he felt a kinship with me because of my surname Brand, which was so common in the Norwegian port from which his parents originated.

At the USO I also met Elena Pavlikowski, a beautiful willowy US/Polish second-generation girl of seventeen, who had long blonde hair in two plaits hanging almost to her waist. If only her brains had matched her beauty, I could have been hooked for life, but one evening sitting on the rocky shore of Lake Michigan with a huge moon shining down on us, our only maintainable topic of conversation was on the subject of films. She was going into great detail of the plot and action of one title when I interrupted to say that I had seen it back home.

"Gee, do you have Movies?" was her reply.

After meeting her family I realised that her intellectual problem was inherited and so ended a beautiful friendship.

A visit to the Chicago Stockyard very nearly converted me to vegetarianism because I was so appalled at the bullying treatment of the cattle and the fear, which I saw in their eyes and heard in their bellows. At the same time I had to concede that, to cope with the volume of beef on the hoof dealt with each day, speed was of paramount importance and merciless efficiency took priority. It also brought home to me how insignificant was the British individual's weekly ration of ten pennyworth of meat plus four pennyworth of corned beef, but continuity of that supply depended upon the existence of places such as this.

Travelling on the elevated railway, I gave up my seat, in a crowded coach, to a black lady in an advanced state of pregnancy, and was taken to task by a huge bull of a man who snarled something like "Say, Limey, if you want to keep your nose clean in this City then you don't stand up for no goddamned trash like her."

As a guest in his country, and in uniform, I took the coward's way out and beat a hasty retreat into the next coach and fled at the next stop, without saying a word but feeling that I had disgraced the British Navy by cowardice in the face of the enemy.

The shops fascinated me with their wealth of variety and their low prices, and I spent a lot of time window gazing, until my legs and abdomen were aching and I sought refuge in the USO where there were always so many interesting people to meet, and so much food and drink to restore lost energy. One evening when I was resting in this comfortable atmosphere I joined in a singsong session where the words were projected onto a screen. The US Marines' Hymn went "If the Army and the Navy ever look on Heaven's scenes, they will find the gates are guarded by the United States Marines", whereupon one of a group of Merchant Navy men who had far too much to drink, shouted "But they'll have to have a British Passport."

All Hell broke loose as a bunch of U.S. Marines set about the Brits who fled ignominiously. I lay "doggo" long enough for everyone present to realise that I was not supporting the ingrates then I got to my feet and apologised for the breach of hospitality and was met with a round of applause, which obviously showed that no offence was taken with the UK, which I represented. The point where a climb-down is effected, is the point where diplomacy is achieved, and I was my country's representative on the spot. I had little choice in the matter.

My visit to the Great Lakes Navy Air Corps Base made me feel full of my own importance, as if I were at least a full-blown Commodore. Piet Larsen introduced me to his station Captain who invited me to be his guest. He was well informed on Taranto and Esmond's Swordfish attack on the Scharnhorst and Gneisenau and he found it difficult to understand why, after three years of war, we had not replaced the Swordfish. I made it clear to him what a desperate position we were in after Dunkirk and described how, at the age of sixteen, I was binding 1914/18 bayonets to broomsticks and making my own version of Molotov cocktails with which to attack tanks. He had not realised the extent of civilian involvement and he also thought that the USA had, without payment, supplied us with arms, armaments and food sufficient for, and even surplus to our needs. I, fortunately, was able to describe the workings of Lease-Lend and expressed our gratitude for, and reliance upon all the support we were receiving.

He quoted Churchill's "give us the tools and we will finish the job" and said he was proud that his forebears were British. He then gave instructions that I was to have the freedom of the Base and he allocated the services of a "Lootenant" to that end.

Never since have I had such an interesting day spent around aircraft. From trainers to Corsairs via Wildcats, Dauntlesses, Kingfishers, Catalinas, even pre-war F4B4 biplanes and Buffaloes. I was mentally worn out and physically exhausted in spite of stopping every twenty minutes for the Coca-Cola "pause that refreshes". I was almost pleased when the time came to "Salute the Flag" at the end of the day and I could go back to the sanctuary of the home of the Bright family.

All good things come to an end, and soon I was enjoying a comfortable club-class train journey back to Toronto, then by local train to Kingston. Back at No.31 SFTS I found that, in my absence, two of my chums who had shared ownership of an ancient Oldsmobile jalopy with me, had failed the course and were on their way back to the U.K. Entrepreneurs, who saw no movement of the car for more than a fortnight, had jacked it up on to bricks and helped themselves to engine, dynamo, starter, battery, wheels, tyres, seats and anything else of value they could see, thinking it had been abandoned. There was some justification for this as, on one occasion, I had driven off while the front passenger door was still held open. Since it was hinged at the rear on to a central pillar, the pillar had broken. As the rear nearside door was mounted on the pillar, the door had dropped and would not close, so we had sawn through the pillar and removed both doors. However the roof missed the support it had from the pillar and sagged to such an extent that we had no choice but to remove the now ill-fitting offside doors and door pillar, whereupon the roof gave up any attempt to support itself so it, too, had had to go. Our then newly-created open tourer was, unfortunately, unlockable and prone to opportunist vandalism. As far as I know, the skeleton still rests at the graveyard end of the airfield car park at Collins Bay.

I had to drop back three courses to No.86 Pilot's course, but such was the camaraderie of trainee pilots, that I was immediately among friends again. Having been away from flying for six weeks I expected to have lost any feel for the Harvard but, in the hands of my new instructor, a huge and gentle Flight Lieutenant from the Bahamas, I had an immediate rapport and suddenly I was completely at home with the controls. Moreover I had used the period of grounding to go over and over all my notes on ground subjects, and the Pilot's Notes handbook for the Harvard, until I was pretty well word perfect. Wonderful Canadian weather allowed me to get three flights per day on many occasions. In a week, we commenced night flying, and after three hours of dual tuition I did my first night solo in the Harvard. I flew to our satellite airfield at Gananoque, which was miles from anywhere, where we lived under canvas for a few days while we did night circuits and landings without inconveniencing our neighbours. Then followed several solo cross-country flights giving a lovely feeling of competence and freedom, prior to extensive instrument flying and a one hour test by the Chief Flying Instructor. This was to check on our suitability to proceed to weapons training and aerobatics. Passing this test was the open sesame to forced landings, low flying, loops, rolls and spins, chase-me-Charlie around cotton-wool cumulus clouds, formation flying, some intensive instrument flying, cine camera work, and machine gunning. The joy of this new freedom was dispelled by a tragedy in which I was involved.

I was detailed for solo night flying and was strapped in my Harvard awaiting instructions to taxi out to take off when a prolonged delay occurred because someone pranged on the duty runway. I had been suffering a rumbling tummy, due perhaps to the effect of hot weather on communal feeding, or the activity of hordes of lakeside flies, and I was eventually forced to call my aircraft handler and ask him to speak to the duty officer with my request for temporary stand-down, which he granted. I climbed out and off I went to the lavatory to my great relief. On returning to the aircraft, I found it had been reallocated to a course colleague, Geoff Fitton, who was already strapped in and receiving instructions to go. I was given the next aircraft, which came in and eventually took off. After doing my stint of nine landings I taxied in and went into the crew room, where I was told that Geoff had disappeared and it was thought that he had spun into the lake on his climb from a take-off. Geoff's brother was on the same course and had to be told.

Next day the wreckage was found and Geoff's body recovered. A Naval funeral was arranged and I was detailed to be a bearer. Standing next to Geoff's brother by the graveside I knew that, by all logic, I should have been the one to be at the centre of the ceremony, and his eyes and mine never met. For the rest of our time at Kingston there was a cloud between us, involuntary and illogical perhaps. Any suggestion of pilot error would have been insensitive, so there was an assumption of mechanical failure meaning that I should have been the one to be "measured for a wooden overcoat" or "go for a Burton" as the euphemisms went. Examination of the wreckage was inconclusive and the tension, was an illustration of how fragile were the strings, upon which our fate and future hung.

I immersed myself in trying to perfect my high, medium and low dive bombing and soon learned the need to release well before commencing to pull out of the dive, as that action lobbed the bomb well beyond the target. By concentrating too much on the aiming, rather than the pull-out, it was very easy to leave it too late, and several times I frightened myself by practically skimming the surface of the lake. I was very thankful that the target did not have superstructure and masts. Dropping simulated depth charges did not require the same finesse, but it was easy to underestimate the time taken for the electrical release mechanism to work, and to find the charges dropping away well after one had passed over the target.

Cine camera gun attacks on an instructor who would rapidly and unpredictably change course, speed, attitude, and height, were great fun. One's aspirations to be an ace fighter pilot were dashed by the difficulty in holding one's fire until really close in case the target got away. Either that or suddenly realising what a mess your propeller was going to make of your opponent's rudder unless you peeled off smartly. Best of all was to machine-gun a ground target such as a mock gun emplacement (which couldn't fire back) and see the spurts of dust leaping into the air. At this stage we felt ready to take on the enemy and all we wanted was to get on with it. How little we knew!

It was now mid-November 1943. The Canadian Fall with its glorious display of maple colouration was nearly over. Our service flying training was complete, with a grand total of one hundred and six hours and twenty minutes of dual instruction and eighty seven hours and twenty minutes solo flying in my log book, and an assessment by the Chief Flying Instructor which read as follows:-

AS A SINGLE ENGINE PILOT	ABOVE THE AVERAGE
AS PILOT/NAVIGATOR	ABOVE THE AVERAGE
IN BOMBING	ABOVE THE AVERAGE
IN AIR GUNNERY	ABOVE THE AVERAGE
HAS HE SHOWN SPECIAL APTITUDE AS A PILOT/NAVIGATOR?	YES
LINK TRAINER INSTRUMENT ASSESSMENT	ABOVE THE AVERAGE

In ground subject examination, largely because of my opportunity to study, I came second on the course. First was Acting Leading Naval Airman Raymond Lygo, who made his career with the Navy, becoming Admiral Sir Raymond Lygo KCB, RN. A worthy competitor, and no disgrace to me in being beaten.

Instrument panel in the cockpit of the North American *Harvard*

Our *Oldsmobile* saloon converted to a "convertible"

The North American *Harvard* in which we all took our Wings Test

The pause that refreshes! (Advt)
L to R: ?Memory fails?, Arthur Lloyd, Ray Lygo, Stanley Brand
Kingston 1943

Chapter Nine
Winged Wonders

My training with the RAF through Service Flying Training School at Kingston Ontario brought me up to the RAF pilot's Wings standard. The opinion of their Lordships of the Admiralty of this hard-won brevet was illustrated by their standard announcement, which went up on our notice board. "Leading Naval Airmen of No.86 Pilot's Course may wear the pilot's badge as from today's date with the following exceptions" - then followed six names. No parade, no band, no brass hat diverted from his important papers to pin wings upon fledgling aviators. We were thus allowed to sew wings on the arm of our uniform, which was of the matelot's bell-bottomed type. We were not granted a Commission at this stage as were winged officer cadets in every other Service of the Allies, and we were not quite sure if this was a ploy to humble us a little in case we got ideas above our station. Or was it so that our return to the UK across the Atlantic could be in steerage below the waterline on a troopship and thus save money? At the same time it would expose us to hardships to which we should become accustomed as a foretaste of life at sea.

We were given seven days' leave, and allowed to change £5 into American dollars which were in very short supply at that stage of the war because the U.K. had to pay for, or obtain credit for, all the supplies which were sent across or sunk in the Atlantic. The rate of exchange was, in 1943, $4.20 to £1. So we hotfooted down to New York with $21 in our body belts and feeling like sovereigns. The hospitality of the United Services Organisation (USO) in New York was quite unbelievable in its efficiency and generosity, providing food, accommodation and entertainment, sightseeing and tickets to shows on Broadway and 42nd Street either free or at very low cost amounting virtually to a booking fee. The ladies at the USO, like their sisters all the world over, were fascinated by our matelot's uniform and badges but when we told them that we were Naval Pilots and translated this into " Navy Air Corps Aviators" we met with complete and utter disbelief. Every patriotic American girl knows that such a hero is made an officer whilst training. Then when he gets his wings they are pinned on his pouter-pigeon chest, (above the proficiency and other medals already awarded), by no-one less than an Admiral with at least three stars, with a three-Squadron fly-past overhead competing in decibels with the massed bands of The United States Marines. Although the girls didn't know what "line-shooters" meant they formed an unfavourable opinion of us and the only way we restored the stars to their eyes was to admit, very convincingly, that we were Carrier Pigeon Operators, First Class. Fortunately the question never arose of how a homing bird knew how far or at what rate of knots its mobile naval home had moved in the bird's absence. Would that WE knew.

At the end of the seven days, we still had enough dollars to buy the essential silk stockings without which we would not dare show our faces back home and then we hitch-hiked our way back to Kingston. It took a few weeks in the transit camp at Moncton, New Brunswick, before we joined our troopship, the new Mauretania, at Halifax, Nova Scotia. With her two short funnels she looked like a slightly smaller Queen Elizabeth in the luxury class of Cunard Blue Riband holders, but how wrong could we be? The Fleet Air Arm personnel were led down through the forepeak to a flat well below the waterline where they sat on kitbags awaiting instructions, which eventually came via an Army lieutenant. He was accompanied by half a dozen soldiers carrying large cardboard boxes which they split open to disclose the contents: individual packs of dehydrated emergency rations. It was explained to us that we would be given one cooked meal each day at 1045 hours, which should be supplemented by two packs of dehydrated rations at whatever times we cared to choose. Copious amounts of liquid must be drunk to avoid the danger of severe constipation inherent with these rations. Each man was issued with twenty meal packs to be carefully guarded because under no circumstances would replacements be made for loss by theft or lustful consumption. We would be allowed on deck for air and exercise for half an hour at 1115 hours each day. Hammocks must not be slung before 2200 hours and must be lashed up and stowed by 0700 hours. Gambling, consumption of alcohol, homosexual activities, theft and brawling were all strictly forbidden and punishable by Captain's decision without appeal. Personnel showing lights or smoking on deck after dark would be charged as aiding the enemy. Parties would be detailed to clean heads (i.e. lavatories) and the mess deck each day. Muster for reporting sick would be at 0800 hours. Water must not be drunk from taps other than those clearly labelled "Drinking Water Only".

More and more troops came aboard and the berth, which we had thought to be reasonably spacious, became crowded, smelly and uncomfortably stuffy. The ship's ventilation even on this bitterly cold December day could not provide and maintain a reasonably cool temperature, low humidity and freshness in the presence of so many bodies. I was told by an off-duty Quartermaster that there were 12,000 people aboard. What a target for Jerry!

My greatest concern arose when I visited the heads, (lavatories) which traditionally were right up in the bows, or heads. Detailing of equipment to troopship standard had obviously been delegated to a junior draughtsman familiar with dockside lavatories but he had never been to sea, or perhaps he had visited the Roman fort at Housteads on Hadrian's Wall and had been inspired by the ingenuity of Roman plumbers. His concept of a latrine consisted of a lead-lined wooden trough about twenty feet long, two feet deep and two feet wide with a time-controlled water inlet at one end and an outlet at the other end fitted with an electric pump which was controlled by the same timer controlling the inlet. There was a gentle fall from inlet to outlet and two wooden beams ran the full length of the trough supporting eight lavatory seats at a splash proof height above the trough. No doubt many of our travelling companions, American troops getting ready for a Second Front in Europe, might have been raised in a hillbilly backwater of the States and were suitably impressed with this multiple closet with running water but, then, their State was landlocked and they could not visualise the Atlantic. The evening before sailing they invented a new form of the childrens' game of "pooh-sticks", consisting of setting fire to paper boats and floating them down the trough under the exposed rears framed above. Worse things were to come.

Our matelot rig made us in great demand when 22.00 hours came and hammocks were slung. Of course we couldn't shame the Navy by admitting that we had never seen a hammock before, and the Yanks thought we were doing a Laurel and Hardy act for their benefit when we got in one side and involuntarily fell out of the other. Most of them would rather sleep on the deck than risk the hammock, but, unfortunately, there wasn't enough clear floor space to go round. It was difficult to make one's way over so many bodies when forced to visit the heads, after drinking the quantity of water required to slake the thirst generated by the dehydrated rations.

Lights out at 22.30 hours resulted in a cacophony of snores and grunts and eventually one made one's own contribution at about 02.00 hours, to be ruthlessly alarmed by the terrifying clangour of the anchor chain falling into the chain locker above our heads. We were under way, confirmed fifteen minutes later by the gentle rise and fall of the deck under our feet as we left the shelter of Halifax harbour. Within an hour there were groans and moans as our landlubber friends were rocked in the cradle of the deep, and found it not to their liking and the retching started. By "wakey wakey" all the sinks in the heads were blocked and the see-sawing troughs were disgorging their fountains of filth in time with the pitching of the ship. In the confined and poorly ventilated space, even the most hardened sailor succumbed to unavoidable nausea. Fortunately the coaming below the doors was high enough to contain the effluent within the heads. A working party of brave men was organised to turn off the water, unblock the drains and sinks then to rig a seawater hose to wash away all effluent. Our rations were stacked on one of the few tables, which saved them from total loss. We dreaded, with very good reason, a December Atlantic gale but our foreboding did not foresee the calamity which lay ahead. It was announced over the Tannoy loudspeakers that some drinking water tanks were contaminated with seawater and the special taps marked "Drinking Water Only" must not be used. Water in uncontaminated tanks would be supplemented with condensate from the ship's distillation unit and would provide adequate supplies for the crossing, provided that rationing was strictly enforced at the level of one pint mug per person, three times a day. I felt that I would welcome anything that would reduce the need to visit that ghastly lavatory, even the combination of dehydrated rations and rationed water, a feeling that I would live to regret. My motionless ordeal lasted twelve days before we dropped anchor in the Clyde but the effect of sixteen days of constipation and resultant anal fissures was to pursue me into old age.

Chapter Ten

Social Graces

The journey from Glasgow to Lee-on -the-Solent, by troop train as far as London, was made tolerable by a break at Carlisle where the good Ladies of the Women's Voluntary Service provided cheese sandwiches and condensed-milk tea which was served in glass jam-jars in case the train moved off with their irreplaceable mugs. At Lee Royal Naval Air Station, where we had joined the Service thirteen months before, we were sent home on leave with travel warrant, ration card, a Naval Officer's identity card and a promise that our Commission Documents and uniform allowance cheque would reach us by post in time to get dressed in our new finery before our fourteen days of leave expired. We would then proceed on a "Knife and Fork" course at the Royal Naval College, Greenwich.

The exigencies of war created a demand for personnel with a level of intelligence, which could not be met in quantity from the strata of society from which the Royal Navy was accustomed to recruit its officer class in peacetime and it was necessary to select brains, which were not necessarily accompanied by the social graces expected of Naval Officers. Now came the opportunity for borderline cases of officer-like qualities to observe and emulate their betters in surroundings and conditions from which they could learn by observation. Jokes were made that we were to be taught not to eat peas off our knife but I countered these with the rumour that due to long practice the best of us could eat peas off a knife when the ship was both pitching and rolling. Whilst our "cabins" were cramped, cold and spartan, because they were the cellar accommodation of the original inmates of the Queen Anne period when the Royal Hospital was built, the service we received from our allocated steward was immaculate, correct and precise, as was his deferential advice. To dine in the "Painted Hall" where Nelson's rum-preserved body had lain in state was an interesting experience, as was observance of all the traditional formalities handed down from the days of wooden ships and wooden-headed Admirals. The impeccable service of the white-gloved Wren stewardesses was a practical lesson in what can be achieved by good training, and the half-naked ladies portrayed on the ceiling displayed the physical attractions of an overseas commission in a warmer climate.

Academically, the contribution of ancient time-served officers as lecturers was very poor, except for an expert in memory-training, who was also an unrecognised case of Alzheimer's disease, (a very interesting combination) but I forget what were the other subjects taught. However, the time passed pleasantly enough and, well-dined, well-wined and cold-bathed, we were next appointed to a land-based training establishment, HMS Macaw at Bootle in Cumberland. It was commanded by Commander Hawkins RN who had been Senior Naval Officer at No. 24 Elementary Flying Training School at RAF Sealand during our course there as trainee pilots. He was a man whom we all respected, admired and held in great esteem for his fairness and firmness and it was a great pleasure to meet him again. We were also delighted to see his bubbly, nubile and pretty secretary who had been commissioned as a junior Wren Officer since we last saw her as a P.O. Wren at Sealand, but her classical poise and dignity prevented rash young sub-lieutenants making advances. Bootle was miles away from anywhere, which did not appeal to us but in due course attracted the Atomic Energy Authority to site their Nuclear Research Establishment there, to the dismay of the locals. Our group hardly had time to unpack our kit and settle in before being sent to No.9 AFU (Advanced Flying Unit) at Errol, Perthshire, where I was to be introduced to the Fairey Swordfish, the aeroplane that was to claim my affection and dominate my outlook on life until my dying day.

Chapter Eleven

Loved One Tries To Kill Me

When the RAF handed the Fleet Air Arm back to the RN in 1939 they did not appreciate the true value of the Fairey Swordfish Torpedo Bomber Reconnaissance aircraft and so let it go to what they considered to be a moribund Service commanded by moribund Admirals, an opinion which may have been justified at the time. Their assessment was that Swordfish were too slow and under-gunned for their purposes, so the Navy could have them, together with those on order. A whole generation of Fleet Air Arm pilots are eternally grateful for the blinkers, which caused this decision to be taken and the British nation should be, too, because what the RAF saw as deficiencies were in many circumstances beneficial in naval operations. Some of the remaining faults were overcome, by the sheer guts and tenacity of Naval Pilots, Observers and Telegraphist Air Gunners, but many of them died because of the incompetence of the inter-war planners and politicians. Nevertheless, the basic training given by the RAF was superb, and this created a wonderful foundation upon which a new generation of Fleet Air Arm aircrew was raised.

The Fairey Swordfish Mk.1 and her younger sibling the Blackburn Swordfish Mk.2 were stalwart, docile, forgiving, tenacious, responsive, manoeuvrable, reliable, slow, sturdy and uncomplicated, which together outweighed the draughts, noise, and lack of urinal facilities. However, nothing could quite compensate for the lack of heating circuits for gloves and Irvin suits except a tropical appointment. These "Stringbags" had Bristol Pegasus XXX engines which would continue to run, in my own experience, even after losing a cylinder head though, of course, for a limited time. They could be fitted with a fixed fine-pitch propeller to give extra power to carry an extra load or reduce take-off run at the expense of high-revving wear and tear and increased petrol consumption. They would continue to fly after losing enormous amounts of wing and control surface fabric through fire or gunfire, and would respond to controls even when on the point of stall. They refused to spin, and would recover from a complete stall by dropping their nose until enough speed was gained to activate control surfaces. They could turn more tightly than any other Allied front-line plane, and could side-slip out of a difficult spot. The Swordfish undercarriage could withstand a heavy landing which would leave a lesser aircraft immobile on deck with its wheel struts pushed up through its wings.

The nickname "Stringbag" was given to the Swordfish because, like granny's string shopping bag, it could always be relied upon to carry things over and above the designed specification. Such extras included, for example, magnetic mines, rocket rails, armour-piercing rockets, explosive-head rockets, rocket flares, searchlights, radar in all its forms, rocket-assisted take-off, cycles and motor-bikes, deep-sea kitbags (extra large ones), and as many as five people in the two back seats going on leave with all their kit.

All the above factors combined to make the Swordfish a very sound aircraft for tasks where it would not meet large numbers of fast fighters, a fact illustrated by the attack on Bomba harbour where three Swordfish sank four ships with three torpedoes; and Taranto, where twenty-one Swordfish attacked the major part of the Italian Fleet. They sank three battleships, two cruisers and two auxiliaries and damaged oil tanks, and other dockyard installations, for the loss of two aircraft and one crew.

The Channel Dash, where six Swordfish without fighter cover perished in the face of overwhelming fighter defence in an attempt to stop the Scharnhorst, the Gneisenau and the Prinz Eugen in their passage through the English Channel, proves the point.

In the 1939-1945 European war zone, this plane sank a bigger tonnage of enemy shipping than any other aircraft. It was the history of the performance of these magnificent machines, and the men who flew them, in those testing days when victories were few and disasters many, which inspired me in 1942 as a boy of eighteen.

Here I was, about to climb into the cockpit of a Stringbag hoping to be worthy of the Elite who had gone before me. It was fitting that on this course I should fly in Swordfish K5661, one of the original batch of three ordered in 1935 subsequent to the crash which wrote-off the experimental private-venture TSR 1 and after the successful prototype TSR2 numbered K4190 was accepted as satisfactory. The other two of the batch, K5660 and K5662 disappear from records in 1938 and 1940 respectively, so I flew the oldest Stringbag of its day, K5661. In years to come I was to fly in a Stringbag ten times the age of K5661 but that is a story to be told later. Although K5661 was retro-fitted with an up-to-date airspeed indicator it had a device fastened to the rear inner port wing-strut, consisting of a 5 centimetre x ten centimetre rectangle of sheet metal fastened to a twenty centimetre length of clock-spring which, in turn, was mounted out from the strut. At the bottom of the rectangle was a pointer reading off a quadrant scaled in knots. The device acted by airflow pressure on the rectangle bending the clock-spring and the pointer then indicated the airspeed. The higher the speed, the greater the deflection. Since the device was not illuminated I wondered if a box of matches was an essential part of the original night-flying equipment? The mind boggles at the problems! The method and accuracy of calibration would be among the more difficult ones.

After flying Harvards, I was surprised to see that we were to be instructed in dual-controlled Swordfish, but then I was also surprised that we had RAF instructors because I had always understood that the Navy took over from the time we achieved "wings" status. Nevertheless, there was a good atmosphere and we settled into a flying programme of three flights each day when weather permitted. It was a good introduction to what the future would hold for the pilot of an open-cockpit aircraft in midwinter. Familiarisation with the type took an hour of dual instruction followed by a twenty-five minute solo check and a one-hour solo flight. The RAF were very thorough in including a great deal of map-reading also navigation depending upon map-reading, which I rarely used again, but enjoyed thoroughly at the time because it gave me the opportunity to discover the delights of the Scottish scenery.

Half way through the course I was given a Swordfish W 5856 which had recently had a major overhaul including re-piping of the fuel system and it had been accepted as O.K. after a test flight. After going through the starting and run-up procedure I turned on to the duty runway and took off.

At a height of about thirty feet my noble Pegasus XXX engine gave two or three alarming coughs and lost power leaving me no choice but to keep going straight ahead whilst rapidly losing height. I turned the three-way fuel cock through all three positions but the still-turning engine failed to pick up. The airfield perimeter fence topped with barbed wire skirted the public road beyond, with a bus trundling towards my line of "flight". Intending to bounce over the top of the fence and bus I stuck the nose down to hit the ground but it was soft after a winter of Scottish rain and my wheels failed to give sufficient of the desired rebound. They then caught the top of the fence and by this time my flying speed had been exhausted so W5856 flipped over on to her back and went tail first into a ploughed field on the other side of the road, missing the bus by feet. Travelling backwards with sufficient momentum to rip off the upper wing, and with it the fuel piping connecting the emergency tank, (housed in the centre-section of the upper wing), with the main petrol tank, we then came to rest. I was trapped in the cockpit, upside-down, ploughed earth everywhere, and with blood coming from somewhere. The petrol tank, (normally below and in front of my feet), was now above me and glugging out its 155 gallons of petrol over me. With petrol getting into my eyes behind my goggles and into my lungs through my microphone-oxygen mask I passed out, but not before I convinced myself that I was on fire. I was told later that an RAF Flight Sergeant got off the bus, scrabbled in the earth with his hands like a dog, then organised others to do the same, until he could reach in to release my harness and drag me out. He then stripped off my entire clothing which was saturated with petrol and he covered me with his jacket and greatcoat. By the time the "blood-wagon" arrived apparently there was little for them to do except to give me oxygen and get me to Sick Bay. In the meantime my saviour collected his own clothes and disappeared without trace.

I woke up, (or was I dreaming?) slumped on a bed with my head cradled on the bosom of a most attractive female who was supporting me with one of her arms around my shoulder. She was trying to persuade me to drink a potion from a goblet, which she held to my lips. As I struggled to activate my arms which seemed reluctant to move in spite of the obvious temptations, her delightful perfume wafted away and was replaced by the stench of petrol, the goblet came into focus as a service pint mug and the elixir which it contained turned into sweetened warm milk to combat the effect of the tetra-ethyl-lead which I had ingested via the petrol. The temptress turned into a pretty WAAF nurse and her boudoir changed into a Nissen-hut ward, close-packed with iron beds. The transformation was made complete with a terrifying clap of thunder and roll of drums as some stupid clot doing load-carrying exercises, taking-off and landing with a dummy torpedo made of 1800 lbs. of concrete, pressed the wrong button and released the dummy to score a direct hit on Sick Bay. It came through the tin roof, landed between two beds twelve feet away from me and buried itself about six feet deep through the three inch concrete floor leaving about three feet sticking up to show that it was a "friendly" missile. There are two versions of my reaction to the incident. One is that I relapsed into that dream-world, which I preferred to reality, by passing-out through sheer funk and the wetness in the bed was not entirely due to a mug of milk being upset in the excitement. Even more derogatory is the second theory adopted by my friends who knew me well, which was that knowingly I took advantage of the diversion, and of the nurse, by burying my head in the cleavage which had tempted me earlier. There is just so much that a man can stand in one day before conceding defeat and I was left wondering what the third incident of the day might be. I soon found out, when, at visiting time I was entertaining my chums with the vision of Heaven, which I had dreamt before reality hit me. Reaction resulted in my voice and laughter getting rather loud, and my lovely nurse heard me say, "I knew I really was in Heaven, because where on earth could you find an angel in, or even out of, a WAAF uniform? She came and threatened me with a carbolic soap enema, administered orally and publicly, which would have been an appropriate finale to my run of bad luck.

Although I was told at the time that W5856 was a complete write-off, like so many crashed Swordfish she lived to fly another day. She was completely rebuilt, this time with a correctly piped fuel system free of air-locks, and shipped out to Canada where eventually she was sold to a farmer in Ontario and then to another in Alabama for crop-dusting. She ended up in crates in Scotland at the Strathallan Collection awaiting restoration, which proved too extensive and expensive for their resources. Acquired by British Aerospace she was reborn to full flying standard and presented to the Royal Navy Historic Flight in 1993. Since then, I have been privileged to fly in her, albeit in the back seat, on several occasions. Having been adopted by the City of Leeds, which has a long history of support to the Fleet Air Arm, including raising nearly ten million pounds in one week in 1941 to fund the replacement of the carrier Ark Royal, W5856 was renamed "City of Leeds". At sixty years of age she is still flying and has another fifty years left in her provided she is restricted to 50 hours of flight per year.

Slow flying, formation flying and night flying completed the course at No.9 Advanced Flying Unit, except for a war game, which involved a dozen of us being driven in a closed lorry at night and dropped singly at a distance of about thirty miles from our base at Errol. All the armed and civil forces were notified of the exercise and attempted to capture us. We were dressed in Navy uniform trousers, roll-neck sweaters and flying boots, had no food, but had two pennies to enable us to make a telephone call if we got into difficulties or wanted to surrender. We were given permission to help ourselves to any Government property but were forbidden to steal any civilian asset and we could speak only as much English as we could German. Under no circumstance must we use violence, but lies and subterfuge were acceptable. All Service transport, including aircraft, were fair game. Our target was to get back to our Flight Commander's office without detection as soon as possible.

Most of us managed to meet up with the person dropped before or after one's own drop, by arrangement, by walking forward in the direction which the lorry went, or back, waiting for up to ten minutes at any intersections. My comrade and I disturbed a policeman in a village, ran off and were pursued by him on his bicycle. We went through a hedge into a clump of trees making enough noise for him to get off his bike, prop it against a gate, climb over and foolishly follow us into the wood, shining a faint torch as he went. We quietly circled round, jumped over the gate, stole the bike and with one on the saddle and the other on the crossbar we peddled furiously, without lights, to distance ourselves as quickly as possible.

After nearly an hour of cycling we spotted an Army unit, which had a small yard or parade ground with a three ton truck parked on it. We went a hundred yards further on, ditched the bike and then crept back silently, looking out for sight or sound of a sentry, but not sensing one we investigated the lorry. My companion, who was Glaswegian and knew about these things, reached in behind the rudimentary dash, pulled out some wires, beckoned me to climb in the passenger side, got in behind the wheel, twisted the wires together and started the engine, then drove us away un-pursued.

Convinced that we were well on the way to finishing the exercise in double-quick time and in maximum comfort, within a couple of miles we came to a shuddering halt in the middle of a winding road and found that we could not restart the engine nor could we change gear into neutral to push the lorry off the road. At the inquest on the exercise we learned that the truck was in a maintenance unit when we stole it, where it was drained of oil from engine and gearbox, but someone had neglected to remove the rotor arm from the distributor. At least my experiences had proved that any escaped prisoner was unlikely to get very far by stealing Service aircraft or vehicles, unless he gave it a major overhaul first.

In the crisp silence which followed our abandonment of the truck and our deliberations of what we should do next, we heard the distant sounds of the shunting of a train, so we set off on a direct cross-country route to find it. This was a big mistake and we learned from it the hard way by getting soaked crossing streams and bogged down in waterlogged meadows. After several hours we learned to stick to by-roads and take the turnings that favoured the general compass bearing we wanted to follow and eventually we found our targeted marshalling yard. Consulting our map we took up a position, by what proved to be the main line to Perth, huddled in some bushes trying to keep warm, chain-smoking cigarettes to appease our hunger and falling into fitful dozes.

The winter-late dawn struggled to dismiss the shadows as we heard a wheezing war-weary and undersized locomotive attempting to spur an over-long train of wagons into reluctantly screeching acceleration. We escapees were feeling a little nervous at the thought of falling under flanged steel wheels through missing our footing in the half-light, unlike the sure-footed American hoboes portrayed in the cinemas of our youth, so a sluggishly moving goods train had some attraction. We had chosen a spot on a right hand bend so the wagons themselves hid us from the view of the driver's cab and the guard's van so we were able to approach close to the side of the train to judge our jump with caution. We were taken aback at the lack of cabin-type vans with welcoming open doors, so we hurriedly settled for a low-sided open truck and clambered aboard. We discovered that the goods in transit were close-packed lavatory pans tightly bedded in straw so we tried to make ourselves as comfortable as possible for the uncertain journey ahead but being hungry and not daring to light a cigarette in a virtual tinderbox, made us feel deprived. At least we knew that our discomfort was transient and would end with a hot shower, a change of clothes and a cooked breakfast washed down with unlimited mugs of tea, whereas real escapees faced being shot, mauled by vicious Alsatians, being beaten with rifle-butts, and put into solitary confinement on crusts of saw-dusty black bread and water. I was awakened from my half-numbed reverie by the insane clatter of a badly adjusted and half-applied hand-brake on our truck and realized that we were coming to a halt. Looking out we saw hordes of troops on both sides of the line, all with rifles and fixed bayonets. We started to clamber out of the truck whereupon a shout went up and our vulnerable backsides were presented to a forest of eager cold steel. Our sympathies lay wholeheartedly with the enemy who, in the words of Corporal Jones in a popular television comedy about the Home Guard was to say "they don't like it up 'em".

B Company of the railway Home Guard, our captors, were cock-a-hoop at their victory of prowess over the local town Company because they, of course, were fighting a different war and were in fact perceived as the real enemy.

We were marched through the streets of Perth, for that is where we had ended up more by good luck than good judgement, as if we were real escapees recaptured, and were actually booed by some old harridans, probably with distant French ancestors who knitted around the Guillotine pausing only when the blade crashed down. At the Police Headquarters we were handed over, and signed for. The Duty Serjeant (Scottish spelling) could not conceal his mirth when told about our theft of a police bicycle by subterfuge, especially after we indicated on the map where it occurred and it just happened to be outside his jurisdiction. Out came his "piece", consisting of cheese sandwiches with lashings of home-made pickle and filled with a layer of raw onion rings, to share with us. The pungent flavour repeated day after day and I remember it yet. His generosity included many mugs of tea from a pot kept on the top of a pot-bellied stove where it simmered constantly. Embarrassed by the lashings of sugar stirred into the tea we were told, with a nod and a wink and "dinna fash yersel," that his daughter worked in a nearby preserves factory where "sugar comes oot yer lugs". Having told where the police bicycle had been abandoned and explained about the Army lorry left blocking a minor road we were put into a Police car and driven in style to the Guardroom at Errol Aerodrome.

Thus ended the No.9 Advanced Flying Unit Course. All pilots destined for Torpedo Bomber Reconnaissance were drafted to the RN Air Station at Inskip near Blackpool in Lancashire.

W5856 as she was in 2003, not as I left her upside down in a field in 1944

Chapter Twelve

Operational Training, or How To Be Offensive

Inskip was the No.1 Operational Training Unit for Anti-Submarine Warfare and we joined 766 Naval Air Squadron. This was our first experience of life in a Squadron, albeit a second-line one, where we were to crew-up with an Observer and a Telegraphist Air Gunner chosen by mutual agreement from about twenty of each. The importance of this selection could not be stressed too highly, as we would be putting our lives in the hands of our crew members on a daily, if not a minute to minute, basis. There would be no room for disagreement, petty quarrels, distrust or breaches of faith, as we would be in close proximity for what might be the rest of our short lives. This in fact proved to be the case for several crews even before advancing to an operational Squadron. After meeting socially on and off duty for a week we were to fly for an hour each with up to six Observers, though at any stage we could mutually agree to stay together with one of our choice. Pilot and Observer then trained together for thirty-five hours of exercises which included, in my case, fifty-five dummy deck-landings by day and night, cross country triangular routes flown without maps as if over the sea, anti-submarine bombing and rocket attacks, formation flying and one of the most important tasks for naval airmen, ascertaining the wind speed and direction. Dead-reckoning navigation uses "the wind" to ascertain the distance and direction between the theoretical position in still air and actual position after flying in moving air for many hours. Over featureless and trackless ocean, a crew, aiming to return to a moving ship in poor visibility, stake their lives on the accuracy of the wind-finding of Pilot and Observer and the correction details of their compasses which they check at every opportunity away from the magnetic influence of ship's steel.

I very soon felt a close rapport with Bill Thomson, a Scot from Methil in Fife, who had a very similar background to mine in that his Father had served in the Army in the first war and suffered badly from that experience, but had still brought up his son with a proud sense of duty and responsibility. Both Bill and I had passed the "scholarship examination" for our secondary education, had matriculated with credit and then, because of the outbreak of war, had consciously decided not to go to University, but to do a useful job, while continuing our education through night school until we were old enough to join the Fleet Air Arm. Flying together immediately confirmed our first impressions of each other and I rapidly realized my good fortune in meeting an Observer so unflappable, so dependable, so trustworthy and so like the brother I was missing so much. Our experiences together over the next year would bond us together even more closely than brothers, if that is possible.

Satisfied with their choice of each other, the embryo crew of Pilot and Observer then had to agree upon the choice of their Telegraphist Air Gunner. This was made difficult by the unnatural barrier erected between Officers and Petty Officers by a hierarchy who, before the days of flight, had no conception of circumstances where specialized training and emergencies could bridge the gap between ranks. Men of the Volunteer Reserve generally had a broader experience of the modern world where these new tenets applied, but such thinking was severely frowned upon by the "straight- laced" regular officers. As a result we had little or no opportunity to meet our air gunners socially, and had to decide our choice along the lines of "Would I care to take this chap home on leave, introduce him to my family and particularly to my sister?" Thereafter his ability to keep in touch with base, to remember to wind in his trailing aerial when coming in to land so as not to decapitate men on deck, to know the difference between enemy and friendly aircraft and ships, to remember the recognition signals of the day in time to stop friends from opening fire, to free a round jammed in the breech of his gun in double quick time, to resist the urge to criticize a particularly heavy landing by screaming out loud instead of inwardly, and more important than all else, to know instinctively, when in desperate danger, whether to keep quiet or to relieve everyone's tension by making an intelligent wisecrack, were the standards by which he would be judged . With only superficial appearances to go by, Bill and I selected three possible candidates and then assessed them on exercises in the air. From them we selected "Taffy", but after several unfortunate incidents we had to decide that he was unstable under stress and we wished to change.

By this time there was little choice, and we took Johnny Hopkins, who looked very young and immature but was enthusiastic about every challenge we gave him, was quick to learn and had an impish sense of humour. A year later, on a dawn patrol guarding a 120-ship convoy in mid-Atlantic, he started to sing "Happy Birthday to Me". He then announced that it was his seventeenth birthday. By then he had been on "Ops" for six months, having faked his age at the recruiting office. I know now that I should have arranged his discharge there and then but it would have broken his heart and destroyed an efficient team. Looking back now, I realize how selfish I was because the stress we were experiencing was too much for a boy of his age, in spite of his surplus of courage.

Inskip became hectic with sometimes four flights a day, supplemented with ground subjects and Link Trainer exercises whenever weather prevented us from flying which became less and less frequent as our experience, ability and confidence grew. I remember Bill repeating his favourite "only birds and fools fly, but no bird would fly in weather like this," when we were fifty miles out in the Irish Sea, but could hardly see our wing-tips.

A submarine was based at Heysham, to operate in the Irish Sea and provide us with a real target for our mock attacks and to give experience to submariners of the latest principles being taught at our Anti-U-boat School. It then became our turn to be the hunted instead of the hunters by joining the sub for a one-day and a one-night exercise. These put me in fear of death by accentuating my innate claustrophobia, even in the absence of depth charges but revealed to me limitations of look-out for aircraft from a sub at periscope depth. Retaliation and mutual admiration were achieved by taking submariners on day and night attacks by Swordfish on their own sub. The course ended with an alcoholic night in the Inskip Wharles

Camp Wardroom, when submariners and aviators Jointly declared a readiness to be shot for cowardice before they would transfer to the other's Service.

Our offensive training was mainly in the use of depth charges and rocket projectiles with solid armour-piercing warheads. Using Air to Surface Vessel (ASV) radar we would home onto a target at night, climb to 1000 feet then, at a range of one mile, go into a steep dive to 500 feet and pull the nose up to fire a single rocket flare over and well beyond the target. This effectively illuminated the target in the "moon path" from the flare and with the Swordfish now in an ideal position to attack, we pushed the nose down, to fire a salvo of six rockets. This method really impressed the submariners flying with us, and gave to them a feeling of grave vulnerability and to us a cock-a-hoop superiority. Alas, experience taught us not to count our chickens because, in every convoy I accompanied there was strict prohibition of the use of radar because of the German development of a means of detecting radar transmissions, which gave away our position. The manoeuvre was never used in action to my knowledge, and we had wasted much time, effort and training opportunity in perfecting it.

Straddling a target with a stick of four depth charges, or sand-filled oil drums for economy's sake, was our main exercise, because weather conditions in the Atlantic would so often dictate a patrol height of less than five hundred feet, which would preclude the necessary dive for a rocket attack. Unfortunately, either our scientific boffins were unable to design an efficient depth pistol, or our piece-working female munitions-workers were thinking more of their encounter with an American GI soldier last night than of the sequence of assembly, because a large proportion of depth charges either failed to detonate, or exploded on hitting the water. Such an explosion, was a little disconcerting for air gunners sitting well aft in a Swordfish travelling at slow speed over the dropping point. A little later in my career when I was Armaments Officer as a duty additional to my flying I complained officially and in writing about the number of premature explosions I had experienced and for my sin

114

I was sent on loan to the Torpedo Establishment at Alexandria in Scotland at the cessation of hostilities in Europe. I was given a Stringbag fitted with the luxury of a radio altimeter, loaded up with an experimental depth charge, which had a pistol activated by the impact of hitting the water and in turn starting a preset timer delaying the explosion by "x" seconds. From Abbotsinch Airfield, now Glasgow Airport, I flew to the range in the Clyde, set the altimeter to one hundred feet and the timer to six seconds as instructed and pressed the release button. Away it went, and exploded on impact. Back at the airfield an inquest conducted by the boffins arrived at the conclusion that the timer had malfunctioned because the impact was too great from a drop-height of one hundred feet, so please would Joe Soap repeat the drop but this time from fifty feet. This seemed reasonable to me and off I went to try again, unfortunately with the same result, and I began to wonder if the boffins were the same ones who had designed the depth-pistol, which had failed so badly during the war!

The diminution of my enthusiasm for cooperation began to show when I was asked to have another go, this time at thirty feet. I agreed to this reluctantly, with visions of a Court Martial sword pointing at me from a table surrounded by top brass should I refuse! However, no miracle came to my rescue and once again off it went. This time, not only did I hear it, the blast came right under my tail-plane, lifting it in the air and consequently depressing the nose of the aircraft to the point where I was heading straight for the "drink". At the same time the elevators were blasted upwards and the joystick thrashed back between my legs, helping to pick up the nose of the 'plane and nothing more permanent happened than the furrows which my under-carriage, then tail-wheel, left in the Clyde. So I thought at the time.

When the singing in my ears subsided weeks later, my hearing was permanently diminished, and the kick in the backside left me a legacy of problems with my spine.

Back at Abbotsinch, when I surveyed the damage to the tail-plane fabric and to the elevators. I laid down the law a little, insisting that anyone asking, nay, instructing me to drop from twenty feet should come along in the back seat, so that he could explain from first hand experience what I was doing wrong to cause the detonation. It was at this point, and with very little deliberation, that the boffins decided to return to the drawing board and I conceded the fact that my awareness of the problem did nothing to provide a solution. But, I digress again and this was all in the future.

It would appear that we were the first course of pilots not to be trained in dropping torpedoes. As we were destined to fly from Macships our targets were assumed to be submarines, against which torpedoes were an inappropriate weapon because one could never be sure of the running depth setting to apply against a target, which would be altering depth rapidly according to the circumstances. Rocket practice and depth charge attacks filled the time when we were not on navigational exercises out of sight of land, and night flying became second nature to us. There were many hazards to be faced and our fatal casualties grew. Nerves began to twang and, after one particular incident, I decided to learn to control myself after giving vent to accumulated temper. Trying to sleep in a Nissen hut in daytime after a long and rigorous night exercise, I was continuously disturbed by the repetitive playing of a gramophone record with the title "Gloomy Sunday". After having my initially polite request to "put a sock in it" totally ignored I became progressively irritated and exasperated and eventually leapt out of my bed, seized the record from its turntable and threw it at the offender, shattering it on the wall of the hut. In the resentful silence which fell after my puerile display of temper I went back to sleep. The crew involved failed to return from their navigation exercise the next day and I hadn't healed the rift. I was too impetuous and too late. Amends must be made at once. Tomorrow's regrets last forever.

Bill Thomson
As he was when we met in 1943   As he was eighteen months later

JOHNNY HOPKINS
After thirteen months in our crew and still under eighteen years

Chapter Thirteen

How To (And How Not To) Land On A Carrier

The grand finale of Inskip's No. 1 Anti-submarine Operational Training School was to join HMS Argus, in the Clyde, to practise operating from a smallish aircraft carrier and to complete fifteen deck landings in daylight and nine at night. At the same time Argus was the finishing school for Deck Landing Control Officers, familiarly known as Batsmen from the ping-pong style of bats held in their hands to make their arm position obvious, who had recently successfully completed a land-based course at Lossiemouth guiding-in pilots to land on a runway marked out as a deck. This exercise was known as "ADDLs" i.e. Aerodrome Dummy Deck Landings, one which had formed a major and important part of the Inskip course but was now to be put into practice in HMS Argus. The Navy was known never to miss the opportunity to use both ends of a rope at the same time and an officer who could devise a way of using the middle whilst the ends were employed was certainly destined to achieve Flag Rank. So, pilots inexperienced in real deck landings and Batsmen with limited experience were brought together in circumstances where catastrophes were surprisingly rare, the credit for which must go to the efficiency of our ADDLs training. In the sheltered waters of the Clyde estuary HMS Argus was reasonably stable so with a little up and down motion at the stern I did two gentle landings, but on the next one, Bats brought me in high and gave the "cut engine" signal whilst I was still about twenty feet above the deck. Obeying the order, for that is the status of a Batsman's command, I fell out of the sky and bounced about fifteen feet up and over the first three arrester wires and with a string of minor bounces, hopped over the rest without engaging the hook and so watched my propeller wrap itself into the barrier.

Fortunately, I had switched off the engine-power as soon as I had started the run of bounces so little damage was done. No blame was attached to me and off I went in another Swordfish. This time Bats brought me in even higher and again gave me the "cut" at a disastrous height whereupon I wilfully disobeyed him, pushed the throttle through the gate, stuck the nose down to pick up safe flying speed then lifted up over the barrier to starboard and went round again to land. This was possible in HMS Argus, as she lacked an island bridge whereas it would have been impossible in a Macship. As I came to a halt a Marine climbed up the side of the Swordfish and shouted in my ear that I must report to the bridge, which was a sunken affair on the foredeck, immediately, at the double. I did so, and arrived there panting and, because of my flying gear, sweating copiously.

Captain Surtees was a martinet who, it was rumoured throughout the Navy, resented the intrusion of aircraft and their occupants on his ship. They were noisy, dirty, came and went at irregular times and tried to govern the ship's movements by their need to turn into wind for take-off and landing. The only way to deal with them was to assert his authority and superiority on every possible occasion. His normal visage was a bilious shade of puce but, as he confronted me, there was a certain phosphorescence about it but not of the cold variety seen in the sea. Volcanic incandescence is a better description. Between his splutters I gathered that, as he assessed himself to be a man of great self control and infinite patience he did not intend to deal with me there and then so he would confine me to my cabin until tomorrow forenoon when a marine would conduct me to the Captain's day cabin. I got the distinct impression that he needed time to find some loophole in King's Regulations and Admiralty Instructions, which would allow him, with impunity, to have me keelhauled, before being prodded by cutlass to walk the plank. All that afternoon, evening and night I dozed fitfully, hearing Captain Surtees-Bligh's voice saying over and over again "Disobedience, Mr. Brand! Disobedience! I will see you hang for this".

Next morning, alone and separated from my course colleagues so there was no one with whom to discuss my predicament, I awaited my summons to His Presence, which came just before noon. "You realise the seriousness of disobeying the lawful order of an Officer senior to yourself, do you?" was his opening gambit. I had no option but to agree.

"Why didn't you obey the way you did the first time Bats made a mistake?" he demanded, throwing me a lifeline.

"Because I too recognised his mistake and I therefore attempted to minimise the damage to His Majesty's property by avoiding the prang Bats was creating" I replied.

"When you have seen as many aeroplane accidents as I have, then and only then will you have the authority to make such decisions but my guess is that you will be Court Martialled, long before you ever get such promotion. Until last week, had I been in your shoes with your limited experience, I think I would have acted as you did, but last Tuesday a pilot did as you did but caught the top wire of the barrier with his hook and crashed into a gun sponson, killing himself and three others so unnecessarily and writing off the aeroplane too. It caught fire and I watched them die and there is no question whether or not a simple barrier prang would have been preferable. Go and bring me your flying logbook because I want to see how your Instructors have assessed your past performance before I decide your punishment."

At the double I returned with my original logbook, together with my new one, which had been started on my first day in Argus. Dismissed and told to wait outside in his anteroom I observed Commander Flying summoned to confer and what seemed ages later the Captain's Secretary ushered me in to Surtees's cabin and I was left alone with him. I was very worried because Senior Naval Officers normally prefer to have a witness to any correct action they may take and only act off the record when some skulduggery is afoot, and according to rumour Surtees was twisted with dislike for all who sailed with him.

"I need a gin" he said, "Will you join me?" All my forebodings were confirmed and he must have seen my whole frame sag.

"Sit down" he commanded and I sat, like a well-trained but cowering dog. There was silence while his steward poured the drinks and the Sword of Damocles oscillated slowly above my head on an over stressed thread. Exit steward and my torture continued. "When you opened up in defiance of Bats, I swore that I would stop that know-it-all whipper-snapper, meaning you, before he kills someone, but, on reading your logbook, I accept that your judgement was soundly based and in no way impetuous. It is to your credit that a wide range of different instructors have assessed you as above the average as a single-engine pilot on every plane you have flown, but this does not entitle you to assess a Deck-Landing Control Officer. That privilege belongs to Commander Flying and myself. It might please you when you hear that the Bats concerned has already returned to his unit for further training, without any blame being attached to him. The blame lies at the door of the person who judged him fit and able to take on the duty of a DLCO before he was ready. Your case is different. If you had obeyed Bat's signal I have no doubt but that a nasty accident would have happened, perhaps even catching your hook on the barrier and killing a gun crew as well as yourself. With little consolation to you we could have given you a funeral with full Naval Honours and no blame attached. However, in the interest of good order and naval discipline I have to ensure that we do not have every Tom, Dick and Harry assuming that they know better than Bats, just because there might have been one occasion where, exceptionally, one person did. Your offence of disobedience will, therefore, be entered in the Ship's Log of HMS Argus and in your Flying Log and you will return to Inskip to gain further experience, rather than for further training. When you return here in one month you will report to me, and refresh my memory because we have rather a lot going on. Now you may go."

I returned ignominiously to Inskip, bearing what had been my nice new and virgin logbook, now horribly defiled, and that rape could be noted by my superior officers for the rest of my Naval career.

I flew up to the Clyde a month later, after the appropriate signal had been sent to arrange my arrival as an individual instead of part of a course, and I searched the Clyde for Argus in good visibility but without success. Lamlash Bay and Dunoon were empty and at about 16.00 hours I found Argus at anchor and swinging into wind in Rothesay Bay with no sign of any life or activity at all. Flying solo without radio or Aldis lamp I had no means of communication. I had my first and only excuse for doing a classic "beat-up" to arouse some activity, but with recent memory of Captain Surtees's wrath, I wimpishly resisted the temptation and waggled my wings instead. Eventually a deck-handling party came out on deck, Bats appeared, the barrier went up and the flying signal was broken out. To my horror it dawned on me that there was no intention of getting under way to provide wind over the deck, which would slow down my landing speed relative to the deck, and then I saw the barrier go down. This convinced me that Captain Surtees was aroused from an afternoon nap or was parted from his afternoon tea and therefore ready for offensive action. Goaded by his anger at the cock-up over an unscheduled arrival signal, he had remembered perhaps that I was due back so had the barrier lowered as a precaution. Full of apprehension I carried out a classical circuit to demonstrate the lowering of my arrester hook, and then proceeded to make the best landing I ever did, even one on a stationary RAF-sized runway. The same Royal Marine as before came running to inform me that Captain Surtees required my presence on the bridge forthwith, and again I lost no time in obeying. When I got there I ran into the slipstream of a full-blast attack on a luckless Yeoman of Signals who had, minutes before, presented his Captain with a signal received two hours earlier. After the furore died away, Captain Surtees suddenly acknowledged my presence, and was profuse in his apologies for his ship's company's shortcomings in making an inexperienced pilot land on a carrier not under way. For one weak moment I was tempted to condescendingly accept his apology but common sense prevailed and instead I crawled with the comment that thanks to him I was now much more experienced. He wished me luck and told Commander Flying to programme me to do fifteen landings next morning "but with a better sprog batsman than last time".

Bill and Johnny joined me via Machrihanish, an airfield on Kintyre, after I had completed fifteen excellent deck landings on Argus with some rough seas running and the deck moving about quite a lot. In six days of intensive activity, we went through the following activities - wireless telegraphy and visual signalling, compass swinging ashore, anti-submarine bombing attacks on a towed target, nine deck landings at night, fifteen by day, two navigation exercises each lasting three hours over sea, five depth charge attacks on towed targets and two on a fixed target, splash gunnery with Johnny's Vickers .303inch machine gun against an aluminium dust marker, two attacks on a moving target first using rockets, then with depth charges, and separate reconnaissance by photographic and visual means of the harbours at Rothesay, Campbeltown, Brodick and Lamlash. We felt as a crew that we were doing, at last, that for which we had joined-up. Commander Flying assessed me and signed my Flying Log "as Deck Landing Pilot, Above Average - 6". Captain Surtees sent for me and his parting words were "I have a reputation for being a bastard but I am a well-intentioned bastard".

I wish I had been able to know him well, because he had the guts and character which were lacking in so many of the old class of privileged public school entrant. I should, at this point, admit that I too was a public schoolboy, but differing in that I was not a boarder. I was a Scholarship day-boy entrant. Both stigmas put me beyond the pale erected by the fear of competition and ability. Surtees knew how to put me in my place and I respected him for it.

Back at Inskip, we were sent on leave which was to be the last visit home for some time, and thereby hangs a tale. It was very late in the day when I caught a train out of Preston by a margin so narrow that I was unable to send a telegram to my parents to let them know I was coming on leave. Reaching Darlington after the last train had left for Middlesborough, my home-town, I decided to leave my kit at the left-luggage office and to hitch-hike home, where I arrived at three o'clock in the morning. Sentimentally I always carried the front-door key on my key-ring and quietly I let myself into the house in complete darkness. Not knowing if the wartime black-out curtains were fully drawn, I decided not to switch on a light, but to undress by the warmth of embers in the open fireplace in the kitchen range. This should have made me realise that something different was going on here, because fuel was too valuable at this stage of the war to allow a fire to have life after ten o'clock at night unless the family were all sitting around it. However I was exhausted and I had stripped off before I remembered that my pyjamas were in a locker at Darlington but I was at home and it didn't matter. I crept upstairs, avoiding those treads which always squeaked, and quietly let myself into my room. I was thinking how I would love to see my mother's face when she found me in bed, after discovering my clothes in the kitchen when she went down in the morning. I climbed into my bed with a lovely scent stirring my nostalgia the way that almost forgotten smells do - and all Hell broke loose. Never in my life have I knowingly given cause to a female to scream so long and so loud. I leapt out of bed, switched on the light and grabbed a towel from the bed-end to conceal my nakedness, as my parents came bursting in through the bedroom door and switched on the light. Sitting bolt upright in the bed, clutching bedding to her bosom was Maudie, the Royal Canadian Army Medical Corps Sister, whom I had last seen one year previously at the Kingston Military Hospital, Ontario, in the emergency when my appendix ruptured.

The Canadian Commando school at Kingston had provided most of her patients, and since these were undoubtedly the toughest, roughest soldiers in anyone's army, Maudie had been compelled to keep them at a distance by developing a reputation as a Dragon who breathed fire and brimstone at the slightest hint of over familiarity, which occurred frequently because she was so regal, so pretty, so caring and so human. Hard-boiled, sweet, with a soft centre was a pretty fair assessment of her nature. Because I treated her with respect and suppressed admiration I'm pretty sure that I received slightly preferential treatment in the recovery ward and so I was the butt of many practical jokes and wisecracks about the Milord Englishman, in a kindly sort of way. Standing in my own bedroom, stark naked until I clutched the towel to conceal my inadequacy under adverse circumstances, trying desperately to explain my innocence, I heard Maudie's explanation for the hullabaloo she had created -"I thought it was your father."

Poor old Dad! He was always the perfect gentleman, and I'm sure he had not looked at another woman since he first met my mother. Mother, teasing, asked Maudie the obvious question "Would you have raised the same hullabaloo if you had known it was Stan?" but couldn't get a direct answer. Dressing gowns donned, we went downstairs to put the kettle on and analyse the sequence of events with a great deal of hilarity.

At Kingston, I had written in Maudie's autograph book and given my parents' address with an invitation to her to contact them if ever in England. Now with a field hospital, she was here in preparation for the Second Front and took up the invitation at short notice. In those days, few households in our district had telephones installed and it was a coincidence that we arrived together. Sleeping on the sofa in our living room was a small penance for me in exchange for the happy family atmosphere created by Maudie's ebullient nature and the bond created between her and my young sister, which lasted for many years.

All too quickly, our time was up and we returned to our units with the knowledge that, for us, our personal participation in the reality of war was about to begin.

The No.1 Anti-submarine School at Maydown near Londonderry in Northern Ireland was the home of the Macship Wing of the Royal Navy containing 836 and 860 Operational Naval Air Squadrons and 744 and 766 second-line Naval Air Squadrons. From this point onwards in the narrative the use of the royal "We" no longer refers to members of a course under training as it did hitherto, but to proud crew-members of the biggest and best Wing of the Fleet Air Arm. It had taken one month short of two years to train for this status.

We soon became aware of the administrative problems of the largest Wing in any of the Allied Forces. With twenty-three flights, each with three or four crews consisting of Pilot, Observer and Airgunner in nineteen Macships sailing east or west or in harbour at Halifax, Glasgow, Liverpool or New York, manning problems were a nightmare in spite of holding a large reserve of about twenty crews. To appoint personnel with the appropriate skills was essential, as every ship had to be self-sufficient in its ability to function in meteorology, armaments, engineering, medicine, photography, stores and spares, pay, safety, parachute packing, aircraft handling, deck landing control, personnel management, discipline, sport, chart correction, King's Regulations and Admiralty Instructions, comforts and protective clothing, entertainments, promotion and welfare, together with all the practical skills of ground crew such as engine fitter, airframe rigger, electrician, radio and radar mechanics, bomb, rocket and depth charge specialists, storemen, etc.. Go to sea without any one of these skills and the ship might just as well turn round and go back, as it could not function correctly.

It was rumoured amongst Macship crews that Maydown's system to deal with this massive task of co-ordination was an equally massive wall chart with pocketed places for all nineteen Macships, twenty-three Flights and 2500 personnel of all skills. Similarly there were cards for all those functions and a knowledgeable team who allocated the appropriate card to the correct pocket. There was a libellous theory, intended to blacken the reputation of people who were unable to give leave because of the demands of the situation in the Atlantic, and a natural scarcity of personnel suitably qualified to be drafted to Macships. It was that the wall chart was so big that it was of necessity close to windows and doors, and during periods of high winds the cards blew out of the pockets and the night cleaners swept them up and carefully replaced them in any pocket where there was an unfilled space.

Shore maintenance back-up team at Maydown
in the cruel winter of December 1944

Chapter Fourteen

The Real Thing, No More Foolin'

After an appropriate period in which we were kept busy doing odd jobs, the Squadron secretary informed us that our crew were to join Q Flight as M3Q aboard the oil tanker Macship m.v. *Alexia*. She would be coming out from behind the Clyde protective boom into the Clyde estuary for exercises within a few days, so we could have a seventy-two hour leave in the meantime so long as we left a contact telephone number and could return to Maydown within twelve hours. As we were unable to reach home but had no knowledge of the best places to stay locally for such a short break we headed for the Padre's office for information. There we were offered a whole range of accommodation from "living it up at all hours" to "rest and relax" at prices ranging from "buckshee" to "pawn the shirt off your back." We settled for the quiet Seabank hotel on the seafront at Portrush, a resort on the Antrim coast, giving ease of access on the same rail route as the Maydown station, and we were delighted to arrive there within three hours of being told we could go.

The Seabank was an Edwardian-style, four-storey hotel with a magnificent view of the sea and the offshore islands called the Skerries. We were made most welcome at reception, by an efficient, but shy, young lady called Reta. She allocated us three magnificent rooms, which we found later, were the best in the hotel even though they were not en suite. Reta told us that there was a patriotic fund, available to aircrew from an operational squadron, which would pay for room and meals but not for alcoholic drinks. We confessed to being new arrivals in the squadron and not yet on ops, but Reta said that our Padre had already taken care of the matter, and I was not to argue. It was a command she was to use at frequent intervals over the next forty-three years.

After an invigorating stroll along the beach and a stick-throwing session with a frenetic Jack Russell terrier, which seemed to have a bottomless reserve of energy, we went in to dinner. We were amazed at the quality and quantity of the food, so much so that we sent our compliments and thanks to Cook, who came into the dining room to meet and thank us in return. Although it was an innocent but well meant gesture, it was the best move we could ever have made, and stood us in good stead whenever we were able to return to the Seabank Hotel between Atlantic round-trips, when we were greeted like long lost sons and fed on the fat of the land.

Next morning, which was a Sunday, Bill, Johnny and I decided to go to church and made ourselves ready in our most "Tiddley" rig. We were on our way out when we met, in the vestibule, Reta and her office colleague dressed in their best and carrying hymn-books. We asked for directions to the Presbyterian Church, to be told that they were on their way there and would we like to go along with them? As Reta said in later years "I've been going along with him ever since!"

After the service and back at the Seabank, I arranged for a pot of coffee and some biscuits to be served for five in a small coffee-room above the main entrance while we all went to our rooms to make ourselves comfortable after our two-hour session on a hard pew. I was the first to take up station in the coffee-room, and it was while I sat there alone that I recalled the wisdom of our mentor at St.Vincent, CPO (Chief Petty Officer) Willmot, who proclaimed, "Them wot is keen, gets fell-in previous". A few minutes later, Bill and Johnny made a brief appearance to say they were going to look for a newspaper. Then came Reta, followed shortly after by her colleague, who said she had to drop out because some guests had decided to leave and their bills had to be made out. So Reta and I were soon left together with the common intent of all concerned that we should get to know each other better. And get to know each other better we did.

Margaretta Lucinda Smyth, known as Reta, was the daughter of William James Smyth, a farmer of Ballymenagh House, Newmills, Dungannon, County Tyrone, Northern Ireland. She had five sisters and one brother. An uncle and his son both served the Presbyterian Church as Moderators of the General Assembly. Two of Reta's sisters were Sisters in Queen Alexander's Imperial Military Nursing Service, two were in the WRNS and Reta was to join the WRNS within a month or two when she reached her 18th birthday. One sister and her brother were too young for the Forces. In total, Reta and I were to spend eleven and a half days together before our engagement and an extra day before our wedding in 1947, but we knew each other so well through our letters during war-enforced separation, that our marriage lasted over forty years and was ended only when she was taken from me in 1987 by the scourge of our times, cancer.

Following our introductory coffee morning, Reta had to go on duty, so Bill, Johnny and I went down to the beach again where we were literally pounced upon by our friend of yesterday, the Jack Russell. He demonstrated his memory by tearing off into the distance to return, panting but game, with a well-chewed stick which he dropped at our feet and then adopted the stance of a sprinter ready for the "off". We walked a couple of miles and, after having the beach to ourselves most of the way, saw a small crowd of people, some of whom started to run towards us. Because of our uniform they thought we were coastguards, for whom they had sent to attend to their discovery, which, we were assured, was an unexploded bomb, at the high water mark. Making reassuring noises we got them to retreat to a safe distance. We felt quite safe ourselves because if it had floated ashore it was not filled with high explosive, and if it had been dropped from a height it would be buried many feet down in the soft sand. It was a finned bomb-shaped object alright, about two feet nine inches long overall and about nine inches in diameter, with a white powdery deposit on much of its surface. It was a smoke-float, of the type we used to mark the spot on a moderately rough sea in the course of determining wind speed and direction. Our reassurance of our audience was endorsed by our doggie pal who, to the applause of the onlookers, cocked his hind leg and peed on the bomb, causing great relief not only to himself but also to all the stressed onlookers who by now totalled about fifty. What to do with the "bomb"? We couldn't leave it where it was or it would go on causing consternation.

The coastguard station was about three miles away, and, with the tide nearly at its height we would soon be walking on the soft sand. With the empty casing of the smoke-float weighing about fourteen pounds we were going to give ourselves a task we could well do without. To my disgrace, I had overlooked the resourcefulness of Johnny, who pointed out the presence of a dozen young boys, who couldn't get close enough to the "unexploded bomb" in case any cameras should be produced to record their bravery for posterity. They would almost fight each other for the privilege of carrying the "bomb." So we set off with the article slung between two boys and the nose of it trailing in the sand because of their lack of height.

By the time we were approaching the town promenade, we were running out of volunteers, but our entourage had grown to about a hundred and the crowd attracted even more people as we went on. As we passed the Seabank, several of the old dears who were long-term residents were sitting in the sunshine in the garden. They asked the fringe of our followers what all the excitement was about and were told that the three young Navy heroes had found an unexploded bomb but " It's alright because they defused it before carrying it off the beach". A little further along we met the Jeep of the bomb disposal squad who were on their way to put a charge under the offensive object and blow it up. The young Lieutenant in charge was quite put out with us for stealing his thunder, and told us that his unit never got any practice, being so far out of Belfast. He was obviously very disappointed when we handed over an empty smoke-float canister. Back at the hotel, we were mobbed by the admiring residents and one old dear even brought out her lacy autograph book for us to sign. The more we protested our innocence of any bravery the more brightly shone our imagined haloes. The incident nearly finished my budding romance with Reta, who feared that it might be thought that her attachment to me was because of glamour or hero-worship, which had not and never would enter her head. All in all, we were delighted to be presented with an avenue of escape when we received a telegram recalling us to our unit. We packed our bags and were on our way even before we checked train times.

The Macship Motor Vessel (MV) *Alexia* was to manoeuvre in the Clyde estuary and take us aboard to complete Q Flight, having taken on replacements for Q1 and Q2 from Machrihanish. There they had swung compasses and had been serviced, while waiting for a slow convoy from Liverpool to assemble and plod up through the Irish Sea to meet our Glasgow section before heading for Halifax, Nova Scotia. At the appointed time we loaded our kit into Swordfish HS375 in her newly painted identity markings M3Q and flew from Maydown to the Clyde, spotted *Alexia* and identified ourselves. Johnny signalled with his Aldis lamp "Hullo, Mum. Orphan seeking adoption. Have you a home for me?"

Alexia replied "Welcome to the workhouse. Mind you don't trip over the step." From our circuit height of three hundred feet I could hardly believe how small she was and how big the step was between deck and sea. Not only that but poking out through the step was the barrel of a four-inch gun which would look me straight in the eye as I approached to land-on. I hoped it wasn't loaded.

I felt an immediate rapport with *Alexia*'s Bats, who kept his bats horizontal all the way in and gave me the "cut" when my wheels were about two feet above the deck and directly over the first arrester wire, which my hook caught and pulled us to a rapid halt. Bats clambered up the side of M3Q and told us not to get out as we were to carry out some exercises detailed on a message-pad, which he gave to Bill. We were pushed right aft and our kit was off-loaded whilst the flight's other two aircraft, M1Q and M2Q, were retrieved from their safe parking area forward of the barrier and ranged one in front, wings spread, and one beside me with wings folded like mine, getting ready for take-off and to do some exercises together. The ground crew and armourer rushed around with two depth charges on a trolley, clambered up to my cockpit to check my "Mickey Mouse" and then loaded the charges one under each wing. "Mickey Mouse" was the nickname given to the mechanical/electrical rotary device, which selected the order and spacing of the release of bombs or rockets. It was so named, after the very popular Mickey Mouse alarm clock depicting the mouse on its face and the clock hands were Mickey's arms. Our device had a prominent rotating arm but on its face in place of hour numerals were terminals connected to bomb release switches. Boys-at-heart saw some similarity and borrowed the name.

It was exciting to participate in what was to be the first of many sequenced take-offs. All three planes ran up their engines and checked for "magneto drop" by switching off one magneto at a time, giving a thumbs-up sign to Bats when satisfied. Bats then signalled to the Air Staff Officer on the bridge that we were ready for take-off. The Skipper, who always took over ship handling whenever flying took place, then instructed the helmsman to turn on to a course, which would bring the ship into wind. A steam jet, issuing at the centre of a protractor painted on the deck, indicated roughly what degree of turn was necessary. When the steam track was about forty-five degrees from the centreline of the ship, Bats started to wind up the first plane to full engine revolutions by rotating his signalling flag above his head. Meanwhile, the pilot held the plane back on its brakes until the deck handlers got a sign "chocks away" from Bats. When the steam, and therefore wind, was straight along the deck, Bats brought down his flag sharply shortly after he felt the deck begin to rise under his feet. The pilot released the brakes and M1Q began to roll, assisted now by a downhill slope turning into a rising bow, anticipating the British invention of the ski-jump deck by about twenty years. By the time M1Q was level with the bridge the bow was rising at its fastest to help lift the aircraft into the air. As the aircraft went over the bow, it had the maximum available height to drop before it would run the risk of bouncing its wheels on wave crests. Immediately after M1Q moved, M2Q was manhandled forward to take its place and position, its outboard wing already spread and the other being opened up and locked in position whilst in transit. Chocks under the wheels, then M1Q's procedure was repeated. During M2Q's run-up, M3Q was already having her inboard wing locked in the open position and was ready to move as soon as M2Q was out of the way. When my turn came in M3Q, my tail was up by the time I reached the bridge but I wondered what it would have been like if my petrol tank had been topped up, if I had four depth charges instead of two, and if the wind had died away as I rolled. The deck was far too short for comfort but, of course, if I was looking for comfort I shouldn't have joined!

"Queenie" flight of three in its new composition, and in a tight Vic formation, did a low level flypast for the team morale of our ship, and then departed for the bombing area. We dropped an aluminium-dust marker and then peeled off in rapid intervals, and each one depth charged it with a single canister dropped by means of the Mickey Mouse which, in anger and reality, would have released a stick of four evenly spaced charges aimed to straddle a submarine. Our seniors planted theirs so close to the target that we thought it would be dispersed before we attacked but we were gratified to see our single one explode just ten yards short of the target, where a following three would have given a perfect straddle with two depth charges on each side of the target. A lethal attack! Smugly satisfied with our performance, but unwilling to return with saved depth charges for fear of a bad landing ending in the drink and causing them to explode in the wreckage by the side of the ship, all three crews repeated the target practice. By this time, the whole area was afloat with stunned or dead fish. Hating to see the waste of good food when it was so scarce, we were pleased to see *Alexia*'s motorboat, already on its way to collect the fruits of the sea, and the spoils of war, to provide our dinners for several days. We then carried out a one hour navigation exercise, checking the accuracy of Queenie Three's compass, my ability to steer a course correctly, our ability to determine wind speed and direction accurately, and Johnny's eyesight in spotting, at the end of the Navex, the remains of a dust marker, from which we took our departure on our triangular route an hour before. No-one could fault our return to within about a quarter of a mile of our starting point and the morale of our three man crew was sky-high, especially after we did three circuits, landings, deck shuffles to move the other two Swordfish, and take-offs, none of which were criticised by Lieutenant George Lyons our New Zealander Flight Commander but were commended by Lieutenant Commander Paton, our Air Staff Officer.

However, I lay in my bunk that night, again visualising a Macship from the air and thought of the sailors' prayer "Lord, thine ocean is so large and I am so small" and in my mind would paraphrase it "Lord, that deck is so small and this plane is so huge".

Settling in to our new life next day was fascinating. We were introduced to our Merchant Navy colleagues, and had to sign the Ship's Articles as Supernumerary Deck Officers in the Merchant Navy to receive our one shilling per month and one can of beer per day in return for which we would accept the authority of the Master over our every thought, word and deed. On signing, our Skipper presented each of our crew with a Merchant Navy badge, which we inserted in the lapel of our RN uniform jacket with pride, knowing full well how horrified regular RN officers would be.

A conducted tour of the ship left us completely confused, and the thought crossed my mind that there would be a major problem to face if, or more likely when, it became necessary to get out of there in a panic, in the dark, listing, with doors jammed, and perhaps with senses dulled with shock or blast. This thought was the best memory conditioner I ever had and wherever I went in the ship from that time onwards, I was always aware of the way out and an alternative. Also, I fastened a torch to a lanyard around my neck where it remained day and night even in harbour. Bill and I agreed never to close our cabin door in case it should be distorted, while closed, to such an extent that we might not be able to open it, so we tied it open with several strands of wire to make sure. We were often quizzed for the reason, and soon saw that many followed our example. We found that a simple curtain served our purpose.

The Purser came to our cabin to see what essential supplies we needed to form our basic working stock of spirits, beer, cigarettes and tobacco. After four years of shortages and ever-increasing taxation we had to control our avarice when tempted by John Haig's Golden Liqueur Scotch Whisky at five shillings a bottle and Senior Service or Capstan Full Strength cigarettes at one shilling for a tin of fifty. To retain a sense of values one must remember that our rate of pay was twelve shillings a day plus six shillings flying pay, out of which we had to buy our clothing and pay for laundry and mess-bills. On an oil tanker there were, of course, strict rules about smoking, which was allowed only in the Saloon, our Briefing Room, and cabins. Nevertheless we all smoked like chimneys and I seemed to broach a new tin of fifty every day, leaving the tin open for everyone to help themselves on an unrestricted basis as common practice. Soda water, tonic and dry ginger were prohibitively expensive because no manufacturer could afford to lose bottles for the price of a deposit, knowing that the cost or non-availability of new bottles at that stage of the war would soon put him out of business, so ship's stores were loaded in price to a level which compelled sea-going types to seek alternatives. Canned soft drinks, plastic bottles and lightweight non-returnable bottles did not exist in those days. For Scots, neat whisky was no hardship, Sassenachs like myself took water with it or else took to the long-standing Navy tipple of gin and Angostura bitters, or the lady guests' usual preference for gin with orange or lime squash. Later, when we skirted the Polar ice barrier the popularity of rum increased dramatically, neat or mixed with anything hot such as tea, coffee, cocoa or even blackcurrant cordial. Beer was never popular, having been tried in very small barrels but resenting the motion at sea, it was barely drinkable. In bottles, it faced the same problem as soft drinks, which was the cost of irretrievable bottles. The development of internal lacquer applied to the inside of cans to resist the attack by beer was still in its infancy and many a can was thrown away hardly touched after the first taste. This was before the days of flat-top beer cans and beer came in the cone-top or 'Mepo' can, so-called after the metal polish sold in that shape of can. Talking to an old friend who served in the Eighth Army in the Western Desert we speculated that somewhere there had been a labelling mix-up because our 'beer' tasted like metal polish whereas their 'metal polish' took the shine off their buttons and there were known cases of 'Doolally-tap', which was a mental derangement caused by years of service abroad in heat and being deprived of women and pubs, where the poor souls actually drank the contents of the cans. Our Purser tried hard to sell us the beer, because his profit was based on the high price, and anyway it had been in stock for several round trips, long before such wares were marked with a sell-by date.

How we enjoyed the halibut mornay, haddock and chips with mushy peas, cod in parsley sauce, bouillabaisse, sole with sauce tartare and unidentified fish rissoles, even when they appeared on the menu for the third time in as many days. Much later it dawned on us that the purser could pocket the value of the victuals, which he was supposed to have bought to feed about one hundred and twenty hungry people for those three days. Provision of a varied and healthy diet didn't come into the calculation. Depth charge discount was a perquisite, which the purser accepted as of right and apparently it was never questioned.

Course of Convoy

I

     I   I

0 0 0 0 0 0 0 0 0 0 0 0 0 0

I   0 0 0 0 0 0 0 0 0 0 0 0 0 0   I

0 0 0 0   (3)   (4)   0 0 0 0

0 0 0 0   0 0 0 0

0 0 0 0   0 0 0 0

0 0 0 0   (1)   (2) 0 0 0 0

   I   I

I

Merchantmen are denoted by (), Escorts by I, and Merchant Aircraft Carrier by ▉. The position (1),(2), (3), or (4) for the Macship within the box was chosen by the Macship Captain, dependent upon the wind direction, to give the maximum run into wind for take-off and landing, clear of other ships.

To turn into a wind coming from anywhere between dead ahead and 90 degrees on the starboard beam, the Macship would take up position (1).

To turn into a wind coming from anywhere between dead ahead and 90 degrees on the port beam, the Macship would take up position (2).

To turn into a wind coming from anywhere between dead astern and 90 degrees on the starboard beam, the Macship would take up position (3).

To turn into a wind coming from anywhere between dead astern and 90 degrees on the port beam, the Macship would take up position (4).

Chapter Fifteen

Saltwater Baptism

We sailed after noon, so that we would be off the coast of Northern Ireland at first light, to join with the Liverpool Section in open water under the umbrella of Coastal Command air cover. Nevertheless, all three aircraft were ranged for a dawn patrol. They were to take off at 0545 hours and sweep 10 miles ahead of the convoy, one to port, one to starboard and one centrally. The sweep was to be five miles on each side of the convoy's course for Queenie One, for Queenie Two five miles on each side of a line parallel to convoy course but offset by ten miles to port, and for Queenie Three a mirror image of Queenie Two but to starboard.

The convoy, totalling fifty-one merchant ships was westward bound for Halifax, Nova Scotia, at a theoretical speed of seven knots. Time was to prove that this was optimistic, as several of the ancient coal burners could keep this up only at the expense of emitting black smoke. This could be a complete giveaway of the convoy's whereabouts, so they had to ease off, and, of course, the whole convoy had to adopt the speed of the slowest. The plucky little corvettes were dashing around like Border collies rounding up an awkward flock of sheep, which resists being told what to do. The main difference was the blasphemy barked out at maximum volume through hand-held loud hailers, the tone of which made interpretation hardly necessary, even for the Greeks, some of whom professed not to speak English except when it suited them. In the confusion and half-light, and with the proximity of Kintyre and Rathlin Island, our Skipper showed off his skill by choosing his position and timing to turn into wind, and let us fly off, without ramming any of the dark shapes looming up from every direction. In these circumstances it is vital that the carrier does not spend one unnecessary second on a course cutting across the track of the convoy. The Squadron record for launching three Swordfish from a tanker-Mac, from being 'steady into wind' to 'helm over to get back on course', was sixteen seconds. The record for landing three Swordfish, from 'steady into wind' to 'helm over to get back on course', was forty-two seconds. In spite of the Macship's pitch and roll we can't have been far from that record on our first operational patrol that dark morning off Northern Ireland. Our team went into action well aware of the hazards we were facing in forming up into the pattern of ships required for the maximum protection of the convoy. The previous page shows the typical convoy layout which forms an open "box" at the centre rear in which the Macship can manoeuvre to ensure that the maximum time is available for flying operations, allowing for the inevitable time-consuming incidents which always seem to occur at the times of the greatest urgency.

Our patrol involved going ahead of the convoy on our search lines flying on a compass course related to that of the convoy, for a specified distance, at a pre-determined speed and for a calculated time. So, as soon as we had cleared the outer limits of our escort we prepared to drop a flame float, to start the essential determination of wind speed and direction at the height we patrolled. This was fifty feet lower than the height where we went in and out of the heavy stratus cloud, so that we were well placed to dodge back into cover if the need arose. Over the next few minutes this is what could be heard over the intercom between Observer and Pilot

Observer: "Stand by to find a wind."

Pilot: "Ready to find a wind." He decides what kind of sea marker is required, whether a flame float at night, or in gloom, a smoke float in rough sea, or an aluminium dust marker on smooth water or on land. He then selects the appropriate bomb via the 'Mickey Mouse' bomb distributor.

O: "Stand by to bomb."
P: "Ready to bomb."
O: "Bomb!"
P: "Bomb gone."
O: "Stand by to turn."

P: "Ready to turn."

O: "Turn!" Pilot turns on to a reciprocal course in a carefully controlled Rate One turn and straightens up.

P: "Turn complete."

O: "Stand by to turn."

P: "Ready to turn."

O: "Turn!" Pilot again turns through 180 degrees in a Rate One turn and is back on his original course, though not over his original position, as the wind speed and direction have borne the aircraft away from this.

P: "Turn complete. Holding original course."

The Observer takes a bearing on the marker at the instant the turn is complete. This is the direction from which the wind has been coming at operational height. He takes a second bearing of the marker after a stop-watch controlled interval. He can now draw a triangle of forces from which he is able to measure the distance which the wind has carried the aircraft downwind, in the measured time, and so calculate the wind speed.

It is quite amazing that with all the inherent inaccuracies, we produced results on which our lives depended, and we survived. Magnetic compasses used for bearings had an unavoidable swinging error, when subjected to acceleration or deceleration in bumpy weather, or a badly executed turn with slip or skid. In aircraft which were tied down to a steel deck for prolonged periods, and at the same time subjected to the vicious vibration of our ship's propeller coming out of the water in rough weather, magnetic compasses were affected by the presence of so much steel, in which magnetism was induced. The huge variations in the earth's field between Glasgow, Greenland and Nova Scotia also had their effect as we traversed the Atlantic. That is why we never missed an opportunity to find a spot on an airfield away from man-made magnetic influences, in order to 'swing our compasses' and correct their errors where possible.

On this occasion we found that the wind speed was eight knots faster and nearly twenty degrees different in direction to the information, probably at least twelve hours old, given to us at briefing. With poor visibility, and radio and radar silence being in force in the Western Approaches the extra sixteen nautical miles, which the wind would have carried us away from the convoy during our two hour patrol, could have cost us our lives by making us run out of petrol, or by flying us into hills if we made for land when we found we had missed the convoy. Of course the latter risk disappears in deep-ocean, but the former risk increases. These thoughts were always present but we tried to banish them to the back of our minds.

The shades of grey intensified after dawn but the horizon was indeterminate, which in an aeroplane gives an eerie feeling of disorientation. This makes the use of the artificial horizon mandatory, however lacking in confidence the pilot may be in his instrument. Constantly one had to fight the urge to fly 'by the seat of one's pants' and this is where hours spent under the hood of the Link Trainer proved to be invaluable in creating an essential trust.

Scanning the waves for a submarine, running with her conning tower low in the water, was not an easy task. The face of the sea had an ever-changing expression, where the deep shadow-grey in the trough between waves would heave itself up into a crest and be transformed into a white horse as the crest toppled, but the grey and white paintwork on a conning tower was unchanging from the day Fritz put down his paintbrush. This was the difference, which we were trying to detect. Amongst the billions of combinations presented for examination within our restricted and badly-lit field of view there might, or might not, be one persistent pattern lurking, to claim the lives of men and ships, and to destroy the vital supplies they conveyed. As we were the one shield between hunter and hunted, one moment of relaxation of sore eyes or tired mind could command a price which we could not afford to pay, via our conscience. So we did our best to fight the cold, the pins and needles and, eventually, the cramp of sitting in one position strapped down tightly, the monotony of engine noise at constant revolutions at low economy speed and the absence of chatter because of radio silence. Great effort was required to prevent the mind from wandering, and worrying, over the things that we could not control. Would the convoy have to deviate from the planned course and speed and so be elsewhere instead of at the arranged rendezvous at the end of our patrol? Would the wind increase to gale-force from the direction of the convoy so that we would run out of petrol before reaching our ship? Would the deck be cluttered with immovable or burning wreckage so we would not be able to land-on? Would those long, rolling waves coming from a direction other than upwind cause the Macship to pitch and roll so much that its unpredictable motion would defeat the skill of our batsman and result in a 'cat-arse-trophic' prang on landing? The mind wanders, to remember the wooden cat-arse-trophy seen in the cabin of my colleague in the form of the rear view of a well-endowed tomcat with a very erect tail, which was handed over in succession to the pilot who currently experienced the most catastrophic calamity, whether or not he was culpable. Doesn't this just illustrate the loss of concentration I was warning about, which may cost lives?

At no time during our patrol, did we see any sign of Queenie One or Two, or indeed any sign of Allied Forces once we got on patrol ahead of the convoy, and, although we were just at the beginning of the Western Approaches to the Atlantic we could already feel the loneliness and immensity of our new habitat.

The monotony of our sweep eventually came to an end when the two-hour stint was up. Although it had seemed interminable, there had been many new and interesting facets to prevent boredom, but the novelty would probably wear off with routine. We turned on to the course that Bill gave me for *Alexia*, and within seven minutes I spotted our leading frigate, and Bill used his Aldis lamp to flash our recognition signal. A few minutes later, we could make out the ship of the Commodore of the convoy, because it was larger than the rest of a very untidy gaggle of ships, belching out black smoke, which streamed out in a rising wind. It was pretty obvious that there was going to be some difficulty in forming up in their correct positions in the convoy pattern, explained by the number and size of the 'white horses' created by the rising wind, and the fact that we were about to lose the shelter which Northern Ireland gave from the storms generated in the Atlantic.

When I spotted *Alexia* a few moments later, and saw the motion of her stern going up and down, and her bridge rolling from side to side, she looked like a surfboard being ridden through breakers by an expert showing off to admiring girlfriends. Only, I wasn't admiring. I was horrified at the impossibility of it all, and I wondered if we had enough petrol to reach terra firma. The more firma, the less terror, was our conviction. Queenie One and Two were circling around and *Alexia* had taken up her position in a rudimentary but imperfect box at the rear and starboard area of the convoy and was turning to port into wind. I opened up the throttle and took a short-cut to formate on the other two in echelon to starboard but, even before I got into position, Queenie One peeled off and started his approach to land-on followed twenty seconds later by Queenie Two. I then did a very tight circuit so that I was in the right position to follow Two at another twenty-second interval. Meanwhile, One was given a wave-off to go round again, then Two landed-on safely hooking the first arrester wire, and I was committed to my final approach. This was on a continuous curve to let me see around the huge cowling of the Bristol Pegasus XXX engine.

I throttled back to reduce my speed, raised my nose and hence lowered my tail and arrester hook, then held this wire-catching attitude by putting on power without increasing my speed, hanging on the propeller. I saw Two taxi forward of the barrier which then went up and it was safe for me to land. Safe? I say again, a purely comparative word. In the North Atlantic it doesn't mean quite the same as it does at home. The bridge had rolled to port at the extreme of its travel and lay in my line of flight. so that it would tear off about six feet of my starboard wings, and the stern was up so high that I must wipe my undercarriage off on the round-down of the deck. Seventy yards to go, and all obstacles started to get out of my way. The deck came down and tilted to become horizontal just as the Batsman brought me in and gave the 'cut'. My hook caught the first wire and anchored me to the deck. The deck handlers poured out of the 'nets', disengaged the hook from the wire and escorted me whilst I taxied up the deck over the lowered barrier. They then folded my wings and parked me well forward protected by the again-raised barrier, by which time Queenie One came thumping down to a safe arrival. Stiff, cold and uncomfortable we climbed down from our cockpits, encumbered by our many layers of clothing and under pressure from our bladders, had a quick word with our ground crew to arrange for immediate attention to any problem, then we made our way to the crew briefing room which had the essential loos en suite.

By the time that all nine aircrew, Bats, the ASO, and the Doctor had assembled, everyone was dying to light a cigarette but, respecting the fact that the Captain was a non-smoker and that the 'Ops. Room' was small, overcrowded and with the threat of fug, refrained until he arrived and said "Gentlemen, you may smoke if you wish". The Skipper thanked us all and congratulated us on the way our first operation of the crossing had been carried out under rather less-than-perfect conditions but went on to say that the weather was deteriorating rapidly and much worse was to come. The convoy had failed to form up satisfactorily and was badly scattered with stragglers all over the place. The escorts needed to be positioned mainly around the line of advance of the convoy so the duty of being 'whippers-in' would fall upon Q flight. For the sake of the new crew, he explained that one of the many great benefits which Macships and their Stringbags had brought to the safety of convoys, was the ability to locate, identify and shepherd stragglers without leaving great gaps in the Asdic defences around the perimeter, caused by the absence of invaluable corvettes or frigates, for days on end. We must be ready to fly off as soon as possible to provide a round up astern as well as scouting ahead of the convoy. All patrols should return to within visibility range of *Alexia* every twenty minutes, so that a recall by Aldis lamp could be given if the motion of the deck became too great or if the speed of the wind coming from ahead of our route should exceed forty knots. Petrol tanks should be brim-full as take-off conditions would be ideal but we had to be prepared for maximum endurance. We were still within striking distance of Eire given a gale-force tail wind when patrolling astern. After we were given details of the stragglers, the debriefing broke up for a meal, consisting of well-filled sandwiches washed down with tea, coffee, or fresh-lemon lemonade. After a session with our ground crew and the reassurance of 'Chiefy', a long-service RAF Flight Sergeant, that all reported defects were in hand, we reassembled in the Ops. room to be briefed for another patrol.

Queenie One was detailed to scout ahead. He was the Flight Commander and the most experienced in heavy weather deck-landing and, at the end of his stint, Eire would be outside his range so even if deck motion were alarming, he would have to grin and bear it. If Queenie Two and Queenie Three (me, the new boy) found themselves too far astern in their hunt for stragglers and, with a fierce headwind which would prevent them from returning to the convoy, they could high-tail it for the land of the Leprechauns. Distance and direction to the nearest land, at the moment five minutes before take-off would be given to both Observers searching astern. And this is where we started in Chapter One.

The experience described in that chapter occurred because of poor visibility, which meant that it took longer than we expected to search thoroughly a given area. At briefing we were instructed to return to the convoy every twenty minutes and communicate by Aldis but this proved to be so restrictive that the instruction was cancelled on the first trip back to the convoy. By the time we found all six stragglers, we were too low on fuel to reach Ireland anyway, and barely made it back to our Macship against the headwind. The end to the episode was disclosed when we were about to leave Halifax at the beginning of our next crossing. At the convoy conference it was announced that the stricken vessel had been found by her resourceful rescuer, which hovered up-wind to create a calm slick and fired a line across, then passed a stronger line attached at their own end to the stern of the ship's boat which in turn had a stout line fastened to its bow. Letting out by the rescuer and hauling in by the rescued enabled the able-bodied survivors to manoeuvre the lifeboat round the bow, which was fairly low in the water by this time, which was the morning after we left her. In this position in the lee of both ships, in spite of the excessive motion the two casualties strapped in body-splints torn from packing cases, were lowered or rather dropped into the hands of the rescuer's volunteers who were manning the boat and desperately fending off collisions with the wreck. All the crew of the distressed ship were taken off, their last duty being to open all the sea cocks to let her sink so as not to be a danger to other mariners. All survivors were brought into Halifax by their rescuer, days after our convoy arrived. However, all's well that ends well!

Escort Carriers enduring Arctic weather, rolling through an arc up to 90 degrees and with stern rising and falling through 50 feet. Macships were smaller and less stable than these, so were dangerously unsuitable for the run to Murmansk, so were restricted to confronting the rigours of North Atlantic extremes.

Escort Carrier *HMS Fencer* rolling 22 degrees from vertical. The same night 40 degrees was recorded on the journey to Murmansk. As *Fencer* was 35 feet longer and 20 feet wider than a Macship it was doubtful whether Macships would have been able to operate aircraft or even to have survived in the weather endured during Russian Convoys.

Chapter Sixteen

What Goes Up, Must Come Down

In Northern latitudes, high winds were among our major problems, and we looked forward to the rare calm periods with some anticipation. Even though halcyon days were a comfort to us, they gave U-boat crews an even greater respite from the ordeal they suffered from constant mildew and the discomfort of wet clothing. We reasoned that, if the wind were too low to provide lift to get us off our miniscule flight deck before we fell into the sea over the bow, then Jerry would be on the surface with all hatches open and everyone, except the engineering watch on duty below, would be basking in the unaccustomed sunshine on deck. With exceptional luck we might even catch them hove-to and with their pants down having a swim. On the Newfoundland Banks, an area of high pressure usually resulted in low winds and fog, or bitterly cold conditions, but these presented problems to Swordfish in gaining adequate lift before running out of flight deck. However, in this region, sunbathing Jerries were as rare as mermaids.

Rocket projectiles, our major war load, whose launching rails interfered with the airflow over the lower wings, reduced the available lift considerably and in light winds it was impossible for a Swordfish to get airborne from the short deck of a Macship. Even discarding all self defence, reducing petrol to half capacity, leaving behind our Telegraphist Air Gunner and fitting a permanently fixed fine pitch propeller were dangerous moves we employed but they were still inadequate. So, for my third Atlantic crossing, rocket assisted take-off gear (Ratog) was fitted, consisting of two rockets each about two and a half feet long and seven inches in diameter, mounted at the rear of the inboard end of the lower stub-wings, and angled so that their thrust was directed through the Centre of Pressure. In theory, Ratog, fired electrically when the aircraft was level with the bridge, would give thrust and lift and send the crew on their way rejoicing instead of sweating with fear. Unfortunately, though the concept of 'environment' was not then in use, it was unkindly and all around us. Rockets sometimes refused to co-operate with the salt water and humidity that formed about 98% of our environment in the Atlantic. When one or the other, or both, rockets failed to deliver what should have been a most welcome kick in the pants, the loss of expected power immediately jeopardised the success of take-off. We would continue to trundle up the deck, carrying a greater load than we would have undertaken without Ratog and could flop over the bow without attaining flying speed. The drop of thirty-two feet from deck to sea might be salvation but that height might not be there if there were high waves. Bouncing one's wheels on wave crests was not something one did out of bravado like a fighter pilot's flick rolls over the duty runway, but it was spectacular and happened with alarming frequency. When both rockets failed, then one's survival depended upon the safety margin employed by the Air Staff Officer in his calculations when he decided whether or not to use Ratog. If he cut it too fine the survivors might qualify for membership of the Goldfish Club which was reserved for those people taking to the 'safety' of a rubber dinghy, or they might get run over by an 8000 ton maritime meat-slicer.

Naturally the ASO made his safety margins as large as possible compatible with circumstances at the time. The cost of the rockets rarely entered into the calculation. If one rocket were to fire alone, the effect depended upon which one it was, port or starboard, and also the whereabouts of the centre of pressure, which moved its position according to the angle of attack of the wings and the lift created at that instant. A force couple was created which would swing the aircraft to the left when the port rocket failed or to the right if the failure was to starboard. In both cases, with insufficient airflow over the rudder and aileron control surfaces, response to the pilot's movement of the joystick was minimal and the aircraft uncontrollable. This at a crucial 'point of no return' and with a swerve leading into the nets or gun sponsons beside the deck, and thence probably over the side into the sea. There was always an urge to apply the boost of Ratog as early as possible, but this desire was tempered by the knowledge that if the port rocket were ignited too early, coupled with the failure of the starboard rocket, the aircraft would swing round to starboard and into the bridge structure. Even under ideal conditions the clearance between bridge and wing-tip was barely five feet, and the impact caused by the swerve would be heightened by the thrust of the active rocket.

If we had been routed down by Madeira or the Azores, or other places where areas of high pressure and hence low winds occur frequently, we could have been eternally grateful for Ratog but we were a little apprehensive because of its unpredictability of electrical circuits in damp and cold weather. The North Atlantic tended to have too much rather than too little wind, the notable exception being the Newfoundland Banks area, with its blanketing fogs. More often than not, fog was encountered on returning to the ship, but departing from the ship in fog was a rarity. Macship aircrew had to be mentally deranged, but we were not so mad as that. The decision lay with the Air Staff Officer, a class of officer whose experience was generally gained in the early days of the war in the Mediterranean, giving them an honest and healthy respect for North Atlantic weather.

Sometimes a really intense fog would lie in a layer only fifty feet thick, and, on one crossing, our convoy gave notice of its presence by two or three greasy black puddles surrounded by grey-white murk, caused by inefficient coal-burning tramps. Close inspection revealed a few feet of mastheads travelling along in the murk, just like periscopes travelling through a pretty calm sea, but without such pronounced wakes. Our masthead was lovingly painted in a fluorescent magenta colour as a result of a similar experience and this was a lifesaver. It gave a less-than-positive indication of the course but, by dint of nerve-racking and dangerous flying, glimpses of the ship could be caught leading to a desperate abandonment of caution and the grasping of the slightest chance of landing whether in one piece or fifty.

To give some idea of how all hands were striving to help, on one occasion when we were airborne in dense fog, ground crew started up both of the parked planes on the bows and revved them up as high as possible to blow down the deck creating a turbulence and trying to raise the air temperature, even if patchy. As one said later "We tried it on because we couldn't bear to think of you stooging around and us doing nowt." They even brought the big signalling lamp off the bridge down to the barrier facing aft and ran a temporary cable to it hoping the light would penetrate the fog and we would see it on our approach. Luck was with us on that occasion, and, with so much help from the deck and a lucky swirl in the fog we were able to make a successful landing. On another occasion in the same area we returned to the convoy at the end of a patrol and ran into dense fog. We spotted a corvette on the outer flank and altered course slightly to head for the 'box' in which our Macship operated and ran into a Brock's firework display consisting of small arms fire, machine gun, Oerlikon and pompom cannon-fire, with and without tracer. We were saved by the swirling fog, into which we disappeared. The offending ship perpetrating this outrage ignored the cardinal rule of convoys by breaking radio silence to announce that bandits had flown into the heart of the convoy. It transpired that it was a U.S. Coastguard escort vessel on its first mission with an international convoy. Hearing an aircraft approaching for quite a number of seconds, (we had slowed down to almost stalling speed to see and be seen with as much warning as possible) the Officer of the Watch had given the order to fire on sight. It mattered not that it was a single engine craft 2500 miles from the nearest enemy airfields! The skin of ship's crew appeared to be in danger, so to be quick on the draw was imperative, in the time honoured frontiersman tradition that the one to shoot first had right on his side. We were lucky that not one of their gunners used the inner ring of his gun sight to aim off on a beam target. Planes just couldn't fly so slowly! As soon as the fog cleared and we flew another patrol we took the galley gash-bin and a pack of a dozen Admiralty toilet rolls with us and anointed our hillbilly sharpshooters, scoring direct hits on their bridge and multiple depth-charge thrower. The latter would be heavily greased against salt-water corrosion so that peas, stew, banana skins and chicken bones would readily adhere to the working parts. The toilet rolls unwound themselves during their fall and three or four clung to the radio aerial and streamed out like paying-off pennants. The ship went into Halifax harbour displaying her disgrace to all that enquired what had happened - and there were many. The Senior Officer of the Escort sent a signal congratulating us on the accuracy of our offensive.

On our first crossing we had an incident, which was a great help in binding together our already stable crew in M3Q. We were nearing the limit of a patrol seventy miles ahead of the convoy about an hour before dusk when I altered my focus from scanning the horizon ahead to scanning my instruments in readiness for a turn for 'home' and in passing I noticed to my horror that the locking handle of the stout pin which held the starboard folding wing in the spread position was no longer held tightly against the leading inboard strut, but was at an angle of about forty-five degrees to it. It had come away from the clip, which should have held it firmly in the engaged position and must have vibrated almost to the unlocked position. We were in imminent danger of the wing collapsing to the folded position where it would cover the cockpits, trapping us so we couldn't bale out, and the other wing, still spread would provide lift on that side only and we would spiral down out of control like a 'winged' grouse. Without any discussion or hesitation, Bill said, "I'll attend to it. Keep her steady".

He spent a couple of fleeting moments, which lasted an eternity, cutting himself a piece of bootlace, which was securing one of his navigating instruments. Divesting himself of his encumbering parachute, within a few seconds he was clambering over my cockpit, hanging on to anything within reach. On the Swordfish, all the designed footholds were on the port side of the fuselage, none to starboard, so to get down the five feet from cockpit rim to the lower stub-plane, Bill had to cut holes in fabric where it was backed up by a longeron or other metal strong enough to take his weight. With foresight, most aircrew carried a knife in a sheath sewn into their flying boot, on a lanyard so that parting with it had to be deliberate.

155

Calmly and coolly, though doing what he was doing would cause a lesser mortal to sweat even in a seventy knot wintry slipstream, Bill inched his way to the strut on which the locking arm was mounted, kicked the handle into the down position, produced his bootlace and lashed the handle firmly in place. Johnny and I didn't cheer until we started to breathe again, and Bill's dazzling white teeth shone from the background of his black beard as he gave a thumbs-up signal. He then commenced his carefully calculated return to the comparative safety of his cockpit where he fastened his safety 'G-string' and clipped on his parachute again.

While all this went on, I kept on flying straight and level, holding my course away from the convoy, reluctant to impose any stress on man or machine until the wing bolt was secure. Thus, we were delayed by about fifteen minutes before I dare turn then another fifteen minutes back, causing us to be overtaken by dusk. The last thing wanted by a Convoy Commodore, a Senior Officer of the Escort, a Macship Captain or in fact any sailor in the middle of the Atlantic with the probability of U-boats lurking around, would be a string of bright lights like Blackpool illuminations to welcome home an errant aircraft. The Royal Navy had always practised the principle of sacrificing the few to avoid risking the many and Bill, who had a fortnight's seniority over me suggested that we must be prepared to ditch near to *Alexia* and trust that we would be picked up, but we would wait and see what provision our skipper made for us to land-on. In fact, as soon as our engine was heard, *Alexia* turned into wind and switched on the dim but lifesaving deck-lights and Bats brought us safely in. The relief shown and expressed by everyone aboard *Alexia* showed what a close-knit family we had become.

Examination of the locking handle disclosed a break in a leaf-spring which held a clip in engagement with a detent fastened to the leading inboard strut. Failure of the spring allowed the clip to disengage and vibration then allowed the handle to inch upwards withdrawing the locking bolt from its socket. "For the want of a nail, the shoe was lost. For the want of a shoe the horse was lost. For the want of the horse the rider was lost, etc."

Many weeks later, on returning to Maydown I reported the incident and recommended that Bill's effort should be recognised as being beyond the call of duty, to be told that it was a case of self-preservation. My reference to the example of Flight Sergeant Hannah, who went out on the wing of his aircraft, a Wellington I believe, and beat out flames with his gloved hands, for which he was awarded the Victoria Cross, was countered with the proposition that if I preferred the traditions of our Sister Service then I should make my application in writing to their Lordships for a transfer to the RAF which would, under the circumstances, be wholeheartedly endorsed by my superior Officer.

With such an attitude prevailing, I made some enquiries and was told that the Officer concerned had been refused a gong for some act of bravery as a Midshipman in Malta. No wonder that 836 Squadron went completely unrecognised. Perhaps another explanation may be that being born so late in the war, 836 had a preponderance of RNVR officers who were not in awe of the old RN hierarchy, and not dependent upon them for long-term prospects of advancement after the end of the war. The frequently expressed irreverence was, I think, feared by a generation of regular officers who had lived through the Invergordon years when the men of the home fleet mutinied, as a possible further source of potential mutiny. Any action that would keep us in our place as an inferior and rebellious mob, would meet with the approval of their Lordships, and any officer with his feet on the ladder beneath them who harboured aspirations of advancement, would be inclined to support them.

Locking handle (red), as seen from cockpit, with wings spread.

Locking
handle

Locating
cone
(female)

Locating
cone
(male)

Locking handle (red), as seen from the deck with wings folded

Maintenance at sea, on the deck of Macship *Alexia*, protected solely by palisades from all the extremes of North Atlantic weather: blizzards, ice, howling gales, salt-water spray, breaking seas, a lurching deck, and a day-long twilight or total darkness during which an ever-vigilant enemy would take advantage of any carelessly exposed light.

Chapter Seventeen
All At Sea

A series of nasty gales persisted in October, November and December of 1944 and made life a misery for the ground crews of the tanker Macships, who had to endure privations of exposure to all that nature could throw at them, with inadequate protection provided by palisades alone. *(See picture of Amastra on page 33 for illustration of palisades)* Swordfish were damaged by breaking loose from their lashings and sliding about on the heaving deck made treacherous by oil spilled during the re-fuelling of our escorts at sea. They slid into their neighbours and we tried to physically restrain them with brute force, by mustering every available man to the task. When an aircraft became too badly damaged, to be repaired on board we had to ditch it over the side if we had other aircraft waiting to land. Whenever there was time we dismantled as much as possible and salvaged undamaged components for further repairs at sea, or for handing over to shore base. For storage at sea, all we had was a large platform abaft the bridge island largely overhanging the ship's side. The platform, called the 'graveyard', was framed with 6in x 6in angle-iron to give it strength, and it had a multiplicity of cleats, on which to anchor the numerous lashings which were needed to hold wreckage securely against the sometimes violent pitching and rolling experienced in storm conditions.

On one occasion, in early 1945 all three of our Swordfish aboard *Empire MacColl* were badly damaged, either when landing in appalling weather or during severe pitching and rolling in the huge swell which followed the storm. As soon as it was possible to work safely on deck, all hands were employed in dismantling wrecked wings, undercarriage, tail planes, engines, etc., and stowing repairable items on our graveyard platform, which was soon chock-a-block. Whilst debating how to accommodate the remaining useable assemblies, I realised that we had enough to make one whole aircraft if only we could fit the pieces together. The ship was still lively and we had no lifting gear beyond a trolley jack and an assortment of pulley blocks and ropes. We also had primitive sheerlegs, which my crew had devised for lifting me out of the cockpit when I was too cold to be able to climb down with the help of their willing hands. We had the ship's radio mast rising up from the bridge island, which we reckoned would take a load of five tons, so what was to stop us from making one good plane out of three wrecks?

The facts that it hadn't been done before, that with the motion of the ship we couldn't even hang a plumb-bob to strike a vertical, that we had no jigs to line-up the angle of attack of wings and tailfin offset to counter torque were arguments put forward and ignored. Brute force in assembly and judgment by eye would have to suffice, and anyway another storm might hit us and write off our hybrid, even before it was test flown. It was at that moment that reality hit me. The thought of the test flight and how our thrown-together and bastard concoction would fly almost made me wish that I had kept my big mouth shut! The only consideration that prevented me from devising insuperable problems or publicly chickening-out from the task was the knowledge that we were the only Macship in the convoy. There was no chance whatsoever of RAF air cover as we were too far from land and the convoy was relying upon us for aerial protection, which we were failing to provide. Anyway, there was so much enthusiasm amongst everyone else aboard the ship that the job would be completed successfully even if I fell overboard, accidentally or on purpose.

Building one flyable swordfish from three crashed ones,
on an open deck in mid-ocean

Stripping down three wrecks into re-useable parts for the
project, valuable spares for stores and rubbish to be ditched

Goofers offered much advice and many opinions,
while their hands stayed warm in their pockets

The useless had to be ditched

They kept me!

Then we started to put the good bits together again

Starting work on Queenie One, we put a strop around the mast with a block and tackle on it. Then, with the aid of a ladder and a long pole, we pushed the strop up the mast as high as it would go. The rope through the block was fastened to the lifting eye provided on the upper mainplane centre-section of all Swordfish for lifting a seaplane version aboard a ship. The strain was taken, enabling Q1 to be slewed around until she was pointing to the side of the bridge. We then fastened a block and tackle between the tail wheel and a stanchion in a gun sponson on the port side of the ship. With many steadying hands on the wingtips of Q1 we able to lift her with the two blocks sufficiently to remove her damaged port wings, port wheel, wheel struts and oleo leg (all for scrap), and to remove the starboard undercarriage complete for salvage. The damaged propeller was scrapped and the splined propeller shaft was padded with a cushion made out of a   bundle of sacks. By repetitive juggling of the ropes through the two blocks, the aircraft was lifted into position with the propeller shaft resting against the side of the bridge structure. In this position there was no danger of the ship's rolling causing damage to the engine by allowing the aircraft to move back and forth with the shaft acting as a battering-ram on the bridgework.

The good starboard wing was then supported on trestle-jacks at a low level and an undamaged pair of port wings was manhandled from Q2, and placed beside Q1 on more trestle-jacks and adjusted for height to be level with the wings on the starboard side. After much jiggery-pokery, letting-out and heaving-in of the two tackles, and grunting and groaning of the hands on the wings, the latter were eventually bolted into place, the locking pins inserted and locked home with the retaining clips. From our previous experience, these clips were closely examined independently by Bill, Johnnie and myself, without collusion or discussion! Q3 was divested of her propeller, complete undercarriage and tail plane, and these were all fitted to the hybrid Q1. We didn't re-number her Q1-2-3 as one wag suggested.

The fitters and riggers then demonstrated their professional pride by asking all supernumery hands to get to hell out of their way to let them check over everything without hindrance or interference. My rigger, with a wry smile, said, "Leave us to it. After all it is your life which concerns us". I knew then that he would not have made such a joke if there was the slightest doubt in his mind, about the feasibility of the action we had taken. My apprehension was reduced a little, for a short while, but then grew alarmingly with the realisation that every man jack aboard ship expected that nobody but

Stanley Brand was going to test-fly this bastard kite of mixed parentage.

We had worked for thirty hours almost non-stop but we spent a short time discussing the project over a meal, and it was decided that I should get some sleep and a shower, allowing one hour for the test flight before dusk, and overnight to correct any defects, if any should be found, so that the plane could be ready in time for a dawn patrol.

Bill Thomson insisted that he was going to come with me, in spite of my protests that it was foolish to expose both of us to risk, because I would not be going out of sight of the convoy, and it was the only time he ever pulled rank;- he had two weeks' seniority over me. Our Flight Commander, Lieutenant Bruce Frame, agreed that Bill should go with me on the grounds that if all was in order, then nothing was lost but if there was a problem, then two minds were better than one.

Ranged right aft with the whole deck stretching ahead of me seemed strange but I went through all my drill meticulously, giving Bats the requisite thumbs-up and the ship started to turn into wind. Bats wound me up to full throttle and as soon as the steam jet blew straight down the deck he sent me off. My tail came up unusually fast, before I was level with the bridge but it was too late to abort. The nose was so heavy that I was afraid the propeller would foul the deck and I wound back the tail-trim wheel to take some of the pressure off the joystick, which I was heaving back into my stomach. I went over the bow and in spite of putting one foot on the instrument panel to give force to my joystick leverage, my wheels touched the crests of several waves. I shouted to Bill to hold tight for ditching as I couldn't gain height and she was terribly nose-heavy. He replied "Don't ditch! I'm going aft".

A few moments later some of the adverse trim eased a little so that I dared glance behind me, to see Bill getting astride the fuselage where the TAG's Vickers machine gun was supposed to be. As it improved further I was able to claw a little bit of height until I was about Macship deck height of thirty-two feet, and again I glanced around to see Bill astride the fuselage out at the tailplane with a handhole cut into the leading edge of the tail-fin, to which he was clinging like grim death until he saw my head turn whereupon he let go with one hand long enough to give me a quick thumbs-up, illuminated by his familiar grin, with white teeth accentuated by his black beard, something I was getting used to seeing under conditions of adversity . All this time I was flying at full throttle and any attempt to reduce power and speed would cause the nose to drop and lose the height, which had been gained at the risk of Bill's life. The concern for our safety on the part of our colleagues made them focus many pairs of binoculars upon us, especially after we dropped over the bow and paddled our feet upon the water "like an obese swan weary at the end of the mating season" as one friend put it. Realising what was wrong and that I needed an emergency return, especially seeing Bill acting as he did, the Skipper of our ship kept into wind while I got round an unorthodox circuit and made my pass at the deck at full throttle with hook down but tail up high. Bats could do nothing except give me 'steady as you go' and then 'Cut' as I came over the round down. Whether the barrier should be up or down under these circumstances was a topic of indecisive conversation for some time afterwards, but my preference would be for it to be up. As there was no way I could go round again I would much rather have wire hawsers wrapped around my propeller and wings than ditch immediately in front of an 8000 ton marine steamroller with a 3,300 horsepower bacon-slicer fitted underneath it.

We caught the fourth wire because fortuitously I came over the stern with the ship horizontal but with the bow rising giving me an uphill run. It was sheer luck that things went well. I had no reserve of power to avoid a rising stern, and if I had hit the round-down or caught an earlier wire, Bill could have been catapulted to his death. Once again Maydown dismissed Bill's action as being self-preservation and hence unworthy of recognition or commendation except that his 'flimsy' (the written assessment of an officer given every six months) drew attention to "his prompt and well-considered response to emergency".

Critical examination of our nose-heavy Q1 creation led to the discovery of an error in reasoning. The angle of attack of the moveable tail plane was adjusted by a rack and pinion activated by winding the tail trim backwards or forwards. In an attempt to replicate the original condition the pinion was engaged in the same number of teeth from the top of the rack as before. However, the trim disc must have been moved to its limit before engagement, making Q1 nose-heavy even with the trim wound fully back to the tail-heavy position. It was a silly mistake, which nearly cost us our lives. This was soon put right and a fresh test flight programmed for dawn, to be extended into a patrol around the convoy at a five-mile radius if all was well.

Bruce Frame undertook this flight to save Bill and me the trauma of a second bite of the apple but, frankly, once we knew the problem and its correction, we would have preferred to finish the job. The test and subsequent patrol went off without incident but that night brought a howling gale, giving me very little sleep because of the need for frequent inspection of the lashings on all of our salvaged bits and pieces, and scaring me to death in the process. We had a fuselage resting on skates and lashed down on the 'graveyard' platform and in the early hours of darkness, it started to move. Over the next ten minutes the movement became so big that it was obvious that a rope had parted. Before the extra strain imposed on the remaining lashings caused them to part, something had to be done. With a coil of rope around my neck and one arm, like a mountaineer, I climbed over the fuselage to get to the outboard cleats intending to fix the rope. When the ship lurched to starboard, the fuselage moved violently as if it was trying to launch into the huge sea which came up towards me, while the heel and sole of my flying boot became crushed between the fuselage and the angle-iron lip around the platform. Fortunately my foot was squeezed upwards and was not trapped, but I hung there, leaning out over the ocean at about thirty degrees, clutching the broken end of a rope hoping that the other end was secure. It seemed an eternity before she rolled the other way, freeing my foot and allowing me to pick up a piece of wood, which I could wedge between the skate and the angle-iron surround to let me replace the broken lashings with the new rope and tighten up. The half-inch diameter rope, which I had secured around my waist right from the beginning, seemed woefully inadequate when I looked at it after clambering to safety. Safety? As I have said before, it is purely relative. Was I safe on the deck of an oil tanker, which looked like an aircraft carrier in the war-torn, submarine-infested Atlantic in the middle of a howling gale? No! As I crossed the deck to go below to the warmth of my cabin, the ship stuck her bow into the front face of a huge wave and scooped up a four-foot wall of water, which came rushing down the deck towards me. I flung myself down on to the nearest arrester wire regardless of the black grease lovingly and copiously applied by the Chief Engineer, wrapped my arms and legs around the wire and tried to wedge myself under it. To this day I am amazed how long it took for four feet of water to pour itself off a flat surface and leave me gasping like the proverbial fish out of water.

Another flight was a visibility-radius patrol around the convoy. I still remember the swelling pride I felt at the sight of the one hundred and thirty ships of which my crew and I were the only protection in the air. There were probably about six thousand men down there, with possibly twenty thousand dependants on shore. The value of the ships and their cargoes ran into a figure beyond my comprehension as the most my wallet had ever held would be around twenty pounds at my then age of twenty two. The ships were irreplaceable and a nation's survival depended upon their continued service, and the contents of their holds and cargoes lashed down on their decks would provide lifesaving support to millions of hungry mouths and weapons of war to our men struggling to defeat the Nazis on the battlefields of Europe. Some responsibility! Here in the year 2004, at the age of eighty-one, I would be reluctant even to lend my ten year old, second-hand car to a twenty-two-year-old man who was a product of the modern society unless I knew details of his upbringing and background. Yet I was fortunate enough to be in the wardroom of HMS Heron at RNAS Yeovilton a few years ago when a flight of Harriers came in from HMS Invincible after serving in the Gulf conflict, and I recognised the continuation of the genes of the Bills and Johnny's in the humour, determination and dependability of

169

the new generation. It must be due to the standards of selection, training and experience imposed by the core of the Fleet Air Arm, which explains this phenomenon. Certainly the esprit de corps is maintained.

I keep drifting from past to present. But was it not always so? The old ex-serviceman sits dreaming and remembering those pals who meant so much to him because those days, actions and circumstances are unforgettable - even those which we would rather not remember because of the hurt, fear and sorrow which goes with them. The damp, watering and cloudy eyes are not due to old age alone. And we are not always fair to the young. To our fathers who fought in Flanders, <u>we</u> were the young, and to the survivors of the Boer war our fathers were young. It was ever thus.

The most intense impression the Atlantic made upon me, was just how insignificant I am in the immensity of this Creation. Why should the concern and interest of the Creator of such magnificence be distracted by some infinitesimal being? The universe is still there when a person disappears forever and there is no alteration. On patrol way out on the beam of one convoy, we saw something miles further out and near the horizon so we altered course to investigate it and realised that it was a ship's lifeboat. It had shipped water or had sprung a leak and lay dead in the water. Dead men lay in the water. Six pitiful remains suffering the indignity of decomposition - bloated and grotesque to the point of disgust yet loved and grieved-for by kin who were still led to believe that "missing" meant there was hope of survival. The world didn't even notice their going, and having gone, the world was not concerned enough to do anything about their remains and left them there for nature to take its course. We were all too busy with mundane matters like our own survival. Sixty years on, the distress and sorrow of bereavement will no longer be the most important thing in the lives of the surviving next-of-kin of those casualties of war and in another ten years the memory of compassion felt by my crew will fade into oblivion as the last of the trio rejoins his friends. And the world will go on without concern. Hurricanes will come and go, fog will come down and disperse, waves will batter and recede, and season will give way to season in all its glory. Constellations will still rotate long after there are no humans left to use them for navigation. The Atlantic showed me how insignificant I am, and created humility in me.

----ooOoo----

Swordfish Mk III equipped with the latest Radar, housed in the "pregnancy" between the undercarriage legs. Two rockets were mounted beneath the fuselage under the pilot's cockpit, for rocket assisted take-off, known as "Ratog".

Chapter Eighteen

Over The Other Side

Halifax, Nova Scotia, was a natural haven and a hive of activity round the clock. The harbour itself sheltered hundreds of ships of every size and age, from the Queen Elizabeth in her regal superiority down to ancient and grubby little coasters. However, we saw little of this if we had a serviceable Swordfish in which to fly ashore as our Macship approached her destination. There was an urgency with surviving and replacement aircraft to swing our compasses at Dartmouth airfield, and to get our servicing completed as soon as possible. Also we had to arrange to replenish fuel, spares, and other consumables as necessary, and remember to take our parachutes in to be aired in the 'hanging-room' under carefully controlled conditions of temperature and humidity to expose or avoid mildew. We then had to re-pack them ourselves, which, we were convinced, was an Admiralty ploy to ensure that we would never have the confidence to bale-out and would therefore increase their chance of us bringing their aircraft home. When all our chores were completed, any time left before our next convoy sailed, was our own. We were never bored with too much time left on our hands.

As soon as possible we would head off into the city to buy stockings, nightdresses, underwear and 'double-barrelled catapults' as brassieres were known. These were the essentials to placate sisters, mothers and even grandmothers, and to keep sweethearts sweet. Too often, delivery in person was prevented by the speed of turn-round of tankers and grain ships preventing home leave, in some cases for up to twenty-one months. Many postal consignments disappeared between Maydown and the UK, with the excuse that Belfast had been bombed.

Our shopping list, governed by the multiple shortages in the UK and our pay of eighteen shillings (ninety pence) a day, consisted mainly of non-perishable food, such as tins of corned beef, bacon, butter, salmon, etc. I found that the most welcomed gift for my

173

family was a ham, whether whole, half, green or smoked, on or off the bone, didn't matter, but on the only occasion that I was at home to enjoy it with them, I found that it had been divided up and distributed among friends, family, and neighbours leaving Mum, Dad, sister Joyce and myself with little but the bone and a mouth-watering memory of what might-have-been, but it made a lovely lentil soup.

In Halifax, any cash left over after our shopping went into the tills at The Green Lantern, a restaurant which served the biggest, most succulent, yet inexpensive T-bone steaks, with all the trimmings such as baby carrots, deep fried battered onion rings and, of course, the ubiquitous french-fries. When the cash finally ran out we retired, either to Admiralty House, or to the wardroom at Dartmouth airfield, where we could sign chits for all our requirements except ready cash. When the crews of two Macships met at Admiralty House there was always great hilarity as they tried to outdo each other in friendly, rough horseplay. The 836 Squadron was so big, and so mobile with nineteen carriers, that the two flights might be meeting for the first time ever or for the first time in eighteen months. Here I must give an example of this isolation. Way back in 1941 I worked with a fellow laboratory assistant, Oliver Jones (inevitably known, with me, as the 'Stan and Ollie' of Laurel and Hardy fame) at ICI. We lost touch with each other when I enlisted as a pilot and disappeared, after which he joined as an observer. In 1998 I appeared in a Channel Four television documentary entitled Classic Aircraft, featuring the Fairey Swordfish, and was seen by Ollie, who wrote to the Television Company enclosing a letter to be forwarded to me, giving me the information that he too had been in 836 and flew from Macships. We had been so close, sometimes arriving at, or departing from, Maydown or Dartmouth within days of each other but totally unaware even that we were in the same squadron. Now, in the 21st century, we keep in close touch to make up for lost time and see each other frequently to set the lamps swinging.

Returning to Admiralty House in Halifax, some evenings ended up rumbustiously in the usual manner of young aircrew letting their hair down in order to relieve accumulated tension, whether they served in RAF or Navy, bomber or fighter, land-based or ship-borne. A degree of irresponsibility countered the overwhelming responsibility thrust upon shoulders which were hardly mature enough to bear the unreasonably huge load bearing down on them for periods too long to endure, without letting off steam. No amount of pontification justifies such actions as borrowing (stealing?) for the night, the twelve pikes arranged in a fan shape on the wall of the ante room of the wardroom at Admiralty House and equipping a guard of honour to march down Barrington Street (the main street in Halifax) to give a display of arms drill with appropriate commands and criticisms in Olde Englishe, as spoken by a drill sergeant of that period. The arms were 'counted back in' by a crestfallen Flight Commander next morning, with a sheepish look on his face.

Our Flight gave a demonstration of make-believe deck landing on a huge rug in the middle of the wardroom, having cleared all the armchairs and tables to the walls. A batsman equipped with ping- pong bats guided a drunken sub-lieutenant, acting as a Swordfish aircraft coming in to land, with many changes of attitude and degrees of urgency. At the last minute of his approach to the 'deck', (which was a long strip of red carpet) he was given a panic wave-off to go round again, which he enacted with enthusiasm, flattening bats in the process. He finally succeeding in landing with a crunch, flat on his face, to be picked up bodily by crowds from the sidelines and rushed up the 'deck' to make way for the next one to land on.

Our visiting sister flight competed with a sketch of what it must be like in a U-boat in the vicinity of a convoy, acting as a submarine Captain giving all kinds of commands in music-hall German to get into attack position. Then, this parody of a U-boat skipper, with the peak of his cap facing the rear, recoiled from his periscope and, with panic in his voice shouted "Achtung! Stringbag!" and headed at top speed for the conning tower escape hatch. This

175

purported to be at the top of a two-inch pipe running from floor to ceiling in one corner of the wardroom, behind a three-seat sofa placed diagonally across the corner and occupied by three senior brass-hats with superior amusement on their faces and gin'n'tonic in their hands. The whole U-boat crew, trying hard to be first up the ladder raced after their Skipper, scrambling madly and roughly over the sofa and occupants and fought tooth and nail with each other to climb the pipe and beat on the ceiling to open the hatch. Anyone other than those on their first visit to Canada knows that Canadian winters demand the comfort of efficient central heating set at a temperature which the average Brit thinks is excessive. This opinion was heartily endorsed by the first of the few who reached the top of the central heating circulation pipe in the corner and their cries of distress sounded quite real. Fortunately, the press from beneath was so great that they found it possible to let go without falling very far, and this minimal fall was cushioned by their supporters and the brass-hats now participating involuntarily. Blisters on both hands and the inside of thighs, were treated by wardroom staff, before we took over treatment by liberal internal application of alcohol which seemed quite effective in suppressing the pain.

On Christmas Eve 1944 we arrived at the Dartmouth wardroom to find the staff had not been notified about the arrival of the convoy on the grounds of security and they were all prepared to go home on leave. We had experienced a particularly stormy and exhausting crossing with the worst November and December gales in living memory and we were ready for a quiet time in different surroundings. We declared ourselves ready to self-cater provided that we were given the keys to larder, refrigerator and bar. This arrangement was readily agreed since they had already completed a stock inventory in readiness for the year-end, provided that we would account for the difference between that and another stock take on their return. Activities died in Halifax that last Christmas of the war in Europe, because it seemed that all Canadians wanted to shut up shop in order to get home to their families. Revelries were dampened by the state liquor laws, which restricted the sale of all intoxicating beverages to the state liquor stores, where the bottles were not only rationed but had to be kept wrapped and unopened until they were safely on private premises. As I have commented several times previously, safety is purely relative. The liquor in the wardroom bar certainly ran the gauntlet of nine healthy thirsts. When all the popular drinks had been consumed by the end of the sixth day, a giant cocktail was created, by mixing all the leftovers and unpopular drinks. These included the rather flamboyant display bottles on the shelf above and behind the bar, such as the nauseous green one labelled crème de menthe, the ruby red sloe gin, the yellow emulsion of egg-nog, and so on. We were very glad to see the return of the wardroom staff, not only to get a hot meal again, but also to see the bar restocked so we could have a hair of the dog that had bitten us.

"What on earth did you do to our display?" they asked.

"If you had left enough of the conventional, we wouldn't have touched it," we replied.

"But it was made with coloured ink!" we were told.

The convoy left a few days later and fog descended almost immediately. The plaintive notes of so many foghorns all in too close proximity made me shudder inwardly as if I was surrounded with lost souls in torment. We still had to go through the motions of preparation for patrols in case we ran into a clear patch, because in these conditions a U-boat would probably feel confident enough to run on the surface. Visiting the lavatory (known as 'the heads' in the Navy because in the days of sail it was up in the bows of a ship, where one could sit overhanging the deep), before a dawn patrol, I happened to intrude upon my flight commander who was gargling with gin, whereupon he swallowed it and then, quite unabashed and unashamed, repeated the dose. His nerve had gone but he didn't want to admit it, and this was his prop to keep him going. The A.S.O. was already aware of the problem and a relief was going to take over when we arrived at Maydown, but the next four weeks were going to be an ordeal and a personal inward struggle for the poor chap. He had done more than his fair share of really active

177

service in Malta and the Western Desert, but pilots with his skill were in short supply and replacements were simply not available. He had to test and train young sprogs like me before he could be released and we knew that we would be treated in the same way, that is, if we survived long enough to become worn out and old like him at the age of twenty-five.

Our Chief Petty Officer, in charge of the ground crew, was dissatisfied with the condition of the engine and electrics of one of the replacement aircraft, Q2, which we had acquired from Dartmouth. This was a very unhappy situation, leaving us with only two serviceable Swordfish for the rest of the Atlantic crossing, and the added encumbrance of having to manhandle the unserviceable one up and down the deck whenever we programmed a landing or take-off. We could of course, dismantle the duff aircraft and park the bits on the graveyard platform. Then the train of thought followed the path of logic. Where could we acquire another serviceable Stringbag? Spare aircraft were held for us at Sydney on Cape Breton Island but we had passed it well on our port beam late yesterday so it must be well over one hundred miles away and getting further all the time. If we did go there and collect a plane, could we get back to our Macship in the convoy or would it be out of range by then? Off we dashed to the Chartroom to consider the problem, and the outcome of our discussion was that one Swordfish, Q1, was tanked up with petrol to maximum capacity and manned by the Flight Commander as pilot, with his observer, his telegraphist air gunner and me, Q3, in the back seat. We took off with Ratog because of the low wind, the extra body in the back, a full tank and the distance to be flown in heavy fog conditions. The unserviceable Q2 would be dismantled and stowed safely away for spares whilst we were away and the deck was not in use. Fifteen minutes after take-off we radioed to Sydney to ensure that a suitable Swordfish would be tanked-up and ready to go. The fifteen-minute delay was to remove us from the convoy in case any fix on our transmission was taken by a U-boat. We went through the process of finding a wind on three occasions in order to reassure ourselves that conditions were stable and without any significant change, which was the case, because on the next leg of

178

our journey, I was going to be without an observer. However, I would have the experienced Telegraphist Air Gunner who would use the radio in emergency, as if transmitting from a shore-based aircraft.

The fog broke up when we were about fifty miles from Sydney and we saw the coastline twenty miles away, enjoying the brilliant blue sky and snow scenery. At Sydney, the RAF had excelled themselves by not only having our replacement aircraft ready but also having a complete set of tarpaulin covers for engine, cockpits and pitot-head stowed in a valise, tied down on the stub-wing. The engine was warmed and there was nothing for us to do, other than climb into the waiting crew wagon to be whisked off to the Officers' Mess, where a hot meal was ready for us, to sit down together with our non-commissioned Telegraphist Air Gunner. This was unheard of in the Royal Navy, but it was everyday practice in the Royal Canadian Air Force on the principle that aircrew were good enough to die together so why shouldn't they dine together? No time was wasted before we went up to the control tower, where a Navigator and a Security Officer were waiting with maps, charts and Meteorological forecasts. Together with Algy, the observer in Q1, they plotted a course back to a rendezvous with the convoy at the new Estimated Time Of Arrival. (ETA) The convoy was heading towards the Newfoundland Banks where, we were told, there was severe fog. The light winds would stay at three to four knots and would be on our starboard quarter, which was a great consolation. In our circumstances, chasing a convoy beyond the point of no return, a thirty-knot headwind would have been disastrous. My walk around the new Q2 was very thorough, as if my life depended upon it, which of course it did. Similarly my cockpit check, and then the engine run-up, and all was satisfactory. She was filled to the brim with petrol and Q1 had also been filled up while we had our meal. I took off five minutes before Q1 and flew around to get the feel and trim and then I formated on him, to starboard so I was not looking into the sun as we were travelling east. In good visibility and with a TAG who had four years of active service experience I was quite happy to hold my position about one hundred yards away from Q1, as they could communicate immediately with the Aldis lamp, and we could get in close to him in a matter of seconds.

After about an hour there were wispy patches of fog around as the cold currents coming down from Labrador round Newfoundland met the warmer and moister air coming up from the east coast of North America and these rapidly became worse until they became a continuous blanket. Naturally, I felt a little unhappy and I closed with Q1 and kept in tight formation on her. After a long period of concentration necessary for close flying I saw Algy stand up in his cockpit and start signalling and I warned my TAG, PO Brotherhood, to start reading what Algy had to say. It was that we were about to pass the point of no return, after which we would have insufficient fuel to reach land, so we would have no choice but to press on to find the convoy however thick the fog became. We replied by asking for an update on the course to the believed position of the convoy and received the answer "course to convoy no change but will tell you any". I checked and reset my gyro-compass and cross checked with the magnetic compass which was badly out, because of the huge variations in the earth's magnetic field in that area. So we pressed on for what seemed an eternity through thick fog, which made me afraid to take my eyes off Q1 for fear of losing her, until my eyes were streaming with tears of strain. Deciding that the cardinal rule that airmen do not go up through cloud because they have to come down again, blind, only holds good where there are cliffs or mountains around, my flight commander Joe, started to gain height and suddenly we broke through not into sunlight, but into most acceptable daylight with a visibility of over a mile all around except downwards. I couldn't help wondering why on earth, at least over sea, that a long service, experienced pilot took so long to do the obvious thing and I could only surmise that his Western Desert experience of sandstorms in hilly areas had conditioned him to a fixed train of thought made worse by his operational weariness. After an eternity, Algy signalled that our ETA was in five minutes, so we knew that we should see the convoy or signs of it within the next few minutes. It was with very great relief that we saw Algy gesticulating towards his port quarter, followed by Joe commencing a very slow circle to port. Neither of us in the new Q2 could see anything to get excited about for quite some time, and then we realised that there were black patches in the fog, with one black pillar rising almost vertically out of the grey blanket. From that moment onwards I would find it difficult to be cross with any freighter making excessive smoke, such was my relief. Relief, however, was premature, as somehow, we still had to find our Macship and then to land on her. Joe led us to the pillar of smoke and then on to a course reciprocal to that of the convoy for a period of ten minutes from passing the smoke-patch. He was aiming for a point astern, where we would be well clear of ships and could lose height safely. We then turned through one hundred and eighty degrees to get back to the convoy and lost height until we entered the fog. A little lower, we caught a glimpse of the sea and Algy could now guess the thickness of the fog bank. By this time, concentrating on staying close to my companion without nudging him, I had lost any ability to keep a mental log of what was happening. We climbed back to a height where we were flitting in and out of murk. Later Algy told me that his estimate was one hundred feet, which was just about ten feet greater than a Macship's masthead. Skimming along the top of the fog layer, now and again we caught a glimpse of a ship and we were able to fly on their course so that, provided they kept in line, we should be able to fly up and down the columns and eventually find our Macship. Incidentally, in conditions like this each ship towed a float behind it on a hawser of such a length that the following ship in its column could keep station on it and know that it was safe as long as two columns did not converge.

The next ten minutes were hair-raising as we came too close to ship superstructures for our own safety. Inevitably one came between me and Q1 and Joe avoided to port whilst I went to starboard and we lost each other in the murk. Talk about feeling lonely in a crowded ballroom. There were far too many folk around, yet no one to hold my hand. Although the convoy occupied an area of about seven miles by three, this was insufficient, for two Swordfish to play blind-man's buff in, so in deference to Joe's seniority I flew up to the front ship in the column and then held my course for a further five minutes to get well ahead of any ships. Doing mental arithmetic more rapidly than ever before, in order to maintain my position, yet let Joe have freedom to find our Macship without interference, I flew in the pattern of a square with steep turns at the corners, but not steep enough to topple my gyro-compass, which would have been disastrous if not fatal. I made the sides of the squares, which were parallel to the convoy course one minute longer than the reciprocal side so that I would hold my position ahead allowing for convoy progress. I thanked my lucky stars for having an experienced TAG in the back seat where he was keeping a log of every course and of the time for which we held it, because he was keeping a vigilant lookout at the same time. He was also keeping a radio watch on our ship's frequency, and he spotted a Very Pistol flare in the colours of the day bursting through the fog layer about two miles behind us. Within another three minutes there followed a green flare and we guessed that Joe was being given the OK to land-on. A note of the bearing was passed to me from the back seat through our communication hatch with an estimate of distance of two miles, so I turned quickly on to the course and started my stopwatch. A few moments later one green followed by two red flares in quick succession soared up in front of us and I reasoned that this meant that Joe was down safely and our Macship had to turn out of wind for safety's sake and go back for another run into wind. Not knowing whereabouts she was in the operating 'Box' I closed up to try to see and to ascertain that it was in fact our own ship and not a very helpful corvette, to be met with red flares and a flashing red light from an Aldis lamp and the ship's signal lamp. We were low enough to see that the ship was in fact what we were longing to see, but we were also low enough to be a danger to ourselves and everyone else as we cut close across her bow, just missing the bridge with our wingtip. At least I was able to guesstimate that her present course was one hundred and twenty degrees to starboard of mine. Mine was 260, therefore hers was about 020, so she was in fact travelling diagonally up the box to reach the North east corner and her final course into wind would be the reciprocal of her present heading, i.e. about 200 degrees. I lifted up to circle above the fog and did some frantic mental arithmetic again. Since the convoy was steering 080 degrees and what little wind that there was came from SSW, approximately 202 degrees. I just couldn't believe it. Two degrees difference after all those approximations just could not be right. There must be a clanger somewhere, so find it, quick! By this time I was getting tired and my reasoning went round in circles, coming back to the same answer each time. My worries were interrupted by a very calm "Green flare bearing Red 90, one thousand yards" from my trustworthy TAG so I turned on to a course of 130 to take us ahead of and across the course of the Macship, skimming the fog-top as we went, rewarded by a jubilant shout of "There she is! Lit up like Blackpool Tower in peacetime". Losing her in the swirling fog I performed the tightest circuit ever, then slowed down until we were hanging on the propeller. With eyes screwed up tight against the slipstream, because I had to push my goggles up out of the way for the sake of clarity, I detected a slight glow in the gloom ahead. Then everything happened at once. I caught a glimpse of Bats feverishly signalling UP and GO STARBOARD at one and the same instant then hurling himself into his safety net as my port lower mainplane sliced through the empty space occupied by his skull milliseconds before. I slammed the throttle closed as my hook caught the first wire and I was clasped to the steel-bound but welcoming bosom of 'mum'. My eyes suddenly felt like red-hot coals and I gave in to an overwhelming need to close them, and found myself being shaken vigorously by Chiefy who shouted to my ground crew "That's what he can do with his eyes closed".

I was practically lifted out of the Swordfish and to my great embarrassment was patted on the back all the way to the debriefing room. After relieving myself and getting a light for the cigarette accepted from several offered I was sitting with my back to the door and didn't hear the Skipper come in until silence fell and everyone stood up. In my cumbersome gear I tried to rise, caught myself off-balance and fell back in the chair, and the Skipper came up behind me and put his arm around my shoulder saying "Don't get up. Welcome back, son", in his warm Tyneside accent, so much like my father (who was born in North Shields) that I had to fight the instinct to hug him in return.

As I relaxed in my bunk that night before dropping off to sleep my mind wandered over all the many separate things which had come together to effect my safe return, and the concern for my well-being, which had been shown by so many people in the action they took to get me down safely. No wonder at my pride in being a member of such a team. If the same esprit-de-corps existed amongst U-boat submariners, and I felt sure it did, then we faced an even harder task than I had visualised.

The next seventy-two hours were spent groping across the Newfoundland Banks in persistent fog, stretching everyone's nerves to twanging point. That is, everyone other than aircrew who could unwind in the knowledge that the fog grounded them except for the need to attack an attacker. As Bill settled down to the updating of some Admiralty Charts he repeated his old adage "Only birds and fools fly and even the birds won't fly in weather like this".

It was too good to last. In the darkness of the night we were roused by the urgent and abrasive agonised groans of the Klaxon, and we put into practice the emergency drills for which we had trained. The raucous voice of the Tannoy address loudspeaker commanded "All hands close up to flying stations. SOE Gnatted (hit by a homing torpedo) Red 20, range five miles".

We arrived at the briefing room short of breath and carrying our clothing which we put on, together with flying kit, whilst the ASO told us the RCN frigate Chebogue, had been hit by a homing torpedo five miles ahead of the Convoy and twenty degrees on the port bow. She had the SOE aboard, and her damage control parties were assessing the situation and trying to save her from sinking. The corvette protecting the starboard flank of the convoy was racing to take off the crew if necessary and air cover was needed in case the rescuer had to heave-to alongside the damaged ship or to pick up survivors. There was still a lot of fog around but patchy in places and so little wind that we would have to use Ratog. Because the breeze was from almost astern we must all move very quickly so that our ship stayed within the Box to present the minimal risk with a U-boat loose around, and possibly within, the convoy. Our ground crews could be heard already running-up our engines and we were ready to go, with depth charges on our racks as we had already decided yesterday that our chances of seeing a U-boat from an attack height of seven hundred feet suitable for launching rockets was pretty unlikely with so much fog around. To carry four depth charges with such light take-off winds and the possibility of rocket assistance failing because everything was dripping wet with fog humidity, we had pre-decided to limit our petrol tanks to one hundred gallons, instead of the maximum capacity of 160 gallons, and also to leave our TAGs behind much to their disappointment. The prospect of a Swordfish dropping over the bow with insufficient flying speed and falling to the depth set on four charges did not appeal to the Ship's Master, and even less to the aircrew.

As we strapped into our places I admitted to myself the hope that this flight might be our chance to catch, by surprise, a U-boat on the surface, and while we were turning into wind I debated with myself the advantages against the disadvantages of wide or narrow spacing between charges. I decided upon thirty feet at a speed of eighty knots. No one was timing the three plane take-off, but it could have been a record with adrenaline pumping through the veins of every man aboard, stimulated with the thought of imminent action.

In the pre-dawn quarter-light we could see the outline of HMCS Chebogue, as she lay still in the water about half a mile ahead of the convoy, with an ugly gap where her stern used to be and twisted, tortured metal all around. There were no signs of any depth charges left in the surviving launchers because they had all been set to safe and ditched. Atlantic mariners knew all too well the effect of underwater detonations on survivors and even new boys like us had seen the belly-up casualties amongst fish too close to the bang. Carley floats and the ship's longboat lay alongside but not tied to her, with one seaman in charge standing by for immediate action, which indicated the seriousness of the damage. Q2 and my aircraft took up prearranged patrols at a radius of 1000 yards from the stricken vessel in case of an attempt to finish her off by torpedo, hoping that we might see the source of the track and thus locate Jerry. Our Flight Commander patrolled right round the convoy at visibility distance, which was now about five hundred yards but very patchy, ready to dash in at any sign of activity.

The corvette from the starboard flank came up and circled the casualty, interchanged a great amount of Aldis lamp talk at such a speed that it was quite unintelligible to us and then a boat was launched from her davit and made its way over to the wallowing and helpless ship with what I assumed was a working party and medical personnel. Meanwhile, a second corvette came up from her previous position on the port flank of the convoy to pick up the SOE from Chebogue so that he could again perform his duties. A line was fired by gun, from the corvette which was going to tow Chebogue, and it was retrieved safely by the working party who then hauled progressively heavier hawsers across and finally took the last and heaviest one through a fairlead in the bow and made it fast to the bitts provided there for the purpose of towing. Gradually the slack was taken up and a ripple was seen at the stem of Chebogue. By this time, of course, the convoy had overtaken the towing and the towed vessels by opening up the width of the appropriate lane, reverting to the original an hour or so later, after passing the corvette towing her wounded companion. Chebogue stayed afloat by dint of skilled and exhausting work by her surviving crew who shored up bulkheads and caulked leaks in riveted plates and put up with buffeting by mountainous seas later in her voyage to Swansea. She had lain like a log in the water because of flooded compartments, which severely reduced her buoyancy and so took a pounding from every wave that hit her. It was heartbreaking for her survivor-saviours to be told, by Admiralty assessors, in Swansea that her frames and keel were so badly distorted that she was beyond repair, so she was taken into deep water and scuttled.

We fully expected that the predator which successfully attacked Chebogue with an acoustic torpedo would be in a position to fire some more inside the convoy and we skinned our eyes for tell-tale tracks for two unsuccessful hours until our parent ship called us in by Aldis lamp to refuel man and machine. Whilst she turned into wind and I positioned myself for circuit and landing I said to Bill "Wouldn't it be just our luck to spot the bugger as we land on?" and Bill retorted "Wouldn't it be just our luck if the bugger spots the Macship before we land on? We will be all dressed up and nowhere to go, I guess"

Q3 was refuelled and re-equipped with Ratog while we downed mugs of kye and wads of corned beef sandwiches. We were ready to fly off again by the time Q2 was recalled and our ship had manoeuvred downwind and turned into wind again. As I got airborne and turned to port, Q2 touched down where I had left moments before so that the Macship could get back on course and safely up front in the Box. This precision was very satisfying, knowing that any weakness in our performance would have left our carrier/oil-tanker and our colleagues vulnerable to an efficient, and no doubt brave, attack on a prime target by a competent and calculating opponent.

We were detailed to patrol the gap, ahead of the convoy, which Q2's landing had created, which was a disappointment to us because by now the submerged U-boat must be inside or abreast of the convoy and our target would have to be a second U-boat, if there was one, ahead of the convoy. That we were trusted to take care of this possibility without any relaxation of vigilance was a consolation in that we were valued members of the team. We noticed the sparks and smoke of the Ratog lifting Q2 back into action, just as Q1 was poised to take her place on deck, and about ten minutes later we were signalled to do a continuous search astern, twenty miles backwards and forwards, at right angles to the course of the convoy on the starboard quarter, starting at the centre-line of the convoy and three miles astern of it. Bill and I discussed this and deduced that we were being positioned to cover the probability of a U-boat, now submerged astern of the convoy, wanting to surface to use its diesel engines at speed, to go round the flank and get ahead, so that it could

187

make another attack. That we were covering the starboard quarter suggested that we were supplementing the escort, which had been depleted by the one corvette towing Chebogue. I couldn't help feeling that in spite of the valour of the crew of Chebogue we should have rescued her crew and sunk the crippled ship so the convoy could retain the towing corvette instead of exposing her and her tow to the enemy and the weather in what must be weeks of slow and dangerous progress with a doubtful ending. They would be limping along, unable to manoeuvre to defend themselves effectively, and I had dipped and waggled my wings in salute to them as they set out on their lonely journey. My feeling that we should never have sent them off was right in hindsight, but it was also felt deeply at the time. I had seen our rescue ship Rathlin rendezvous with Chebogue and I had circled around at a range of about one thousand yards as they lay stopped in the water whilst five stretcher cases were transferred to the care of the professional medical team in Rathlin. We then had to get on with our duty. We had seen Q1 go off to the port quarter on a line reciprocal to ours and we guessed that Q2 would be going round and round the convoy at visibility distance.

So the day dragged on, but we were given progressively longer breaks between patrols so we could take a few turns up and down the deck to stretch cramped legs suffering from poor circulation, then have a smoke and shut our eyes for a blissful twenty minutes. Before dusk we changed our tactics and probed deeply with patrols out on the flanks and ahead. If only we had been allowed to use Radar we might have caught our adversary but it was not to be. We had wanted revenge for Chebogue, and were not content with a passive or preventive function. It was pretty dark when we finally gave up and not one of us suffered the ordeal of insomnia that night, though instead of sleep-dust we felt we had handfuls of sand in our eyes. We were very lucky that the visibility had improved progressively, so that for most of the day we were within sight of either the convoy or escort. We knew well the value of the reassurance given by companionship in the wastes of the Atlantic.

----ooOoo----

The greatest demands on the skill and judgement of a Macship pilot came at the end of a long winter patrol: when he had to face the difficulties of landing back on to a tiny heaving and rolling deck. His mind and body would be frozen after hours in an open cockpit exposed to a 72 knot wind exacerbated by the eddies of propeller slipstream. Lack of any facility to provide warmth during the prolonged immobility of being strapped down against the bumps of turbulence, coupled with the eye-watering intensity of the strain of searching in half-light for the tell-tale signs of a semi-submerged U-boat in broken water, made human error inevitable and accidents unavoidable.

Chapter Nineteen

Just Routine!

The weather continued to improve and visibility on our dawn patrol next day was around twenty miles from one thousand feet. There was no chance whatsoever of catching a U-boat on the surface, but we were achieving our purpose to make them impotent and slow by forcing them to submerge and keep away from our convoy. And so it went on day-after-day, getting colder and colder, as the winter anticyclone kept up with us. The second hour of a two-hour patrol became agony as our circulation slowed down, creating numbness in our fingers and toes and our brains suggested sleep as an antidote to the misery. Nature worked on the metabolism of selected animals, so that these conditions caused hibernation to protect the beasts from the environment, but our society prevented us from lapsing into such comfort. The slipstream from our whirling propeller came corkscrewing around the fuselage, into our open cockpits and whipped away any little pocket of undisturbed air which might harbour a few degrees of warmth, so we became colder and colder and colder. The air temperature dropped to well below zero, but the wind-chill factor must have been at least twenty degrees below that, in the seventy-knot slipstream around the open cockpits. The rubber mask, intended for oxygen but never used for that because a height of above ten thousand feet was hardly attainable, and in any case operationally unnecessary, gave some little shielding from side draught and also carried our intercommunication microphone but it also acted as a condenser for the only warm thing left, our breath. The condensed moisture sought its way by capillary attraction into the contact area between skin and rubber and froze there and while sealing off the draught, it deadened the feeling of the skin so that when the time came to remove the mask, the skin was removed too. My cheeks, chin and nose lost the top layer of skin in this way, and damned painful it was, making shaving an impossibility and use of the mask an irritant torture for many weeks. Hairs growing through the broken skin created an indescribable itch to add to the misery.

Describing my appearance at this time my kinder friends said that I resembled a rat peeping out of a haystack and they altered the name on my cabin door to 'Brushwood Brand'. Anyone craving sympathy should avoid joining the Air Branch of the Royal Navy.

The 'rig o' the day' became fairly standard. It started with pyjamas, retained because of reluctance to strip down to the buff after the warmth of bed. On top of these went silk long john underpants to insulate and to protect against the itchiness of the next layer, called "Scapa Scanties", which were woollen long-john underpants, topped by a long sleeved vest or vests. Then came a woollen roll-neck sweater with battle-dress trousers and jacket followed by a one-inch-thick quilted kapok flying suit, and over all of this an Irvin jacket and Irvin trousers made of sheepskin leather with the fleece turned inwards. The Irvin suits were wired for electric heating but the extra electrical load for three of us was deemed to be too great for the standard Swordfish generator. I could never get an answer to my request for a generator with increased capacity. Leather helmet, padded goggles, silk gloves under woollen gloves under leather gauntlets, woollen scarves knitted with the love of dear ones or silk articles of underwear used as a scarf to demonstrate prowess in the cause of Venus, woollen socks, long oiled-wool seaboot stockings and fur-lined flying boots completed the regalia. With so much insulation, the trouble was that once the cold found its way in, it stayed there, without any chance of respite.

A further problem was that since none of the fly-zips lined up with another, the meandering path through four-inches thick of various layers of clothing came to about fifteen inches so that even the most boastful aviator was defeated when it was necessary, nay imperative, to pass water. The urge to do so took complete charge of one's mind as soon as the need arose, because of the awareness of the impossibility of fulfilment. Our one hope was that one of the pipes in the waterworks would freeze without flooding the basement, painful though it may be. Although that never happened to me, I did have leakage which was cold, uncomfortable, smelly and unhygienic and caused salt-water boils on the inner thighs where chafing occurred.

To extricate me from my cockpit after a two-hour stint in temperatures such as these, my ground crew constructed sheer-legs on locking wheels, which they could trundle to position a block and tackle above my cockpit. It was fitted with a big hook which they hitched to a strop looped under my armpits and fastened to my parachute harness so they could hoist me, like King Henry the Eighth being lifted from his warhorse on return from the battlefield. My main regrets are that this was before the days of amateur cine-cameras, and that I was not in the best position for taking snapshots either. As a tribute to my fitness in those days, dressed like the Michelin man in the tyre advertisement, I was always able to clamber up the steep side of the Stringbag, while encumbered by a parachute, over the cockpit coaming, which was about eleven feet above the deck, and get into my seat without assistance. But getting out unaided was quite impossible once aviator rigor-mortis set in. Frequent freezing and thawing damaged the tissues of my feet and legs, ruining the circulation and storing up problems for me in later life. At the time and later, on demobilisation, I was so thankful to be alive there was no thought whatsoever of claiming any compensation or pension for what proved to be a handicapping disablement. The same attitude applied towards the rupture of my eardrums caused by faulty depth charges. How different to the rush for the financial cure-all demanded in modern times.

Halcyon days generally called for uneventful patrols at long range, hoping at least to be seen by the enemy if we failed to spot him first, with many changes of course to avoid providing a pointer to or from the convoy. Under these circumstances, and with three serviceable aircraft, we could cover a huge area of ocean. When we had one or more aircraft unserviceable, the three crews took it in turns to fly whatever was available and utilised their free time to catch up on their supplementary duties, many of them pleasant but all of them demanding of time and concentration. Chores complete, sleep took the next priority, then sports to maintain our fitness (this was challenged by our Quack, who had to deal with lacerations, contusions, sprains etc. as a result of our enthusiastic approach to deck hockey). Pursuit of hobbies came next, then socialising which included debate on religion, politics and the opposite sex. We knew that 'Officers and Gentlemen' were supposed to bar such topics in the wardroom, but we opted out of those categories because it was a civilian saloon anyway, and the topics were much more interesting than any of the wardroom conversations we had experienced previously. It was this attitude of the real world that we experienced in later years at University, where it would have been ridiculous to veto a subject from discussion just because an ignoramus might want to get embroiled in fisticuffs, which was the Naval fear. We would be pleased if he would expose himself as a contributor to the theory of might over right, so we could assess the worth of his opinions on other matters. As a result we came across many amusing anecdotes. Have you heard the one about the Bishop and the Actress?

Hobbies were multifarious, ranging from ogling what was then considered to be pornography, but now enters family homes with impunity disguised as page three of a national tabloid newspaper. We read anything from a Mickey Spillane to Gibbon's Decline and Fall of the Roman Empire, and practised handicrafts, such as the needlework of our huge, ham-forearmed and callous-fingered Tyne-sider First Mate. He embroidered fifteen-inch-wide FAA wings in red, white, blue and gold across the chest of a sweatshirt, which he then wore on every possible occasion, even to a Masters' Pre-Convoy Conference. Ashtrays made from shell-cases, and letter-openers from Swordfish bracing-wires, showed the ingenuity of acquisitive instincts. My own interests were model making, metal turning and making a photographic enlarger from a bottle-glass lens salvaged from a broken signalling lamp. I was often quizzed as to why I was not studying Maths, Physics and Chemistry to give me a flying start at the second half of my BSc London external degree and, frankly, I hadn't got the answer ready. Even if I survived until then, about which there was some doubt, would I still want to study? Wouldn't I hate to go back into a laboratory where the results of one's efforts might not be discernable for one or two years and where I would have to submit to the opinions and instructions of someone much younger than myself who had never taken a decision involving life or death? Would I find it easy, or even possible, to defer to someone who had accepted the status of a reserved occupation and had cocooned himself inside that protection, while he accumulated seniority and salary increases with acquisition of status? Frankly, the prospect appalled me. How about a Permanent Commission? Would I fit in with the old RN? Or with the peacetime RN? Would the new RN pick its officer class against privilege or ability considerations? I still had the words of the brass hat at my Selection Board ringing in my ears, "And do you ride"?

It still rankled with me. I was convinced that he was not astute enough to be devious in his intent, but that he really thought it mattered. In his assessment, a boy whose parents could provide an opportunity to ride a horse was ipso facto superior to a boy whose parents could not. I thought of my Uncle who earned his Military Cross on the Somme by storming a machinegun post, which had wiped out more than half of his platoon. He was wounded but back with his platoon remnants in the same trench within four weeks. He had to earn his living after the war by emigrating to Canada where he sold, intermittently, vacuum cleaners and brushes from door to door. Or my father, twice mentioned in despatches in 1915 and 1917, still suffering in 1928 from the effects of poisonous chlorine gas, having to stand deferentially at the gates of Smiths Dock at six o'clock in the morning, hoping to be allocated one day's work by a foreman who had been an apprentice when my father joined up in August 1914. Earning one day's pay would debar him from one week's dole money. Would things be any different this time?

The alternative would be as bad, if the extreme left got its own way. My sister-in-law served in Queen Alexandra's Imperial Military Nursing Service from the beginning of the war in 1939. She went through the fall of France, and would have been on the Lancastria when it was dive-bombed and sunk with great loss of life, except that she volunteered to stay behind in France to prepare men who were badly wounded to travel. Later she served in India, and on

195

her return to the U.K. arrived in the middle of a Southampton dockers' strike. Her kit, and that of her contingent, was not allowed to be unloaded from the troop ship. She had to waste days of her disembarkation leave before being allowed to collect her belongings.

The attitude of our Merchant Navy stewards and the ship owners endorsed my feelings. Extreme Left and extreme Right were so selfish that they did not care who was hurt or damaged in the course of getting their own way as long as they achieved their ends. Where is the support for the benefit of the common good? My attempts to find my God in the Churches which professed to be led by Him, had been a dismal failure, but what I had found is that the world is full of lovely, wonderful people, like Bill, Johnny and many others aboard the ships in which we served. If the parable of the talents is anything to go by, there are so many talents worthy of reward that great riches are in store for them, but in this world the benefits all seem to go to the wrong people. But, then, who are we to judge? All I can say is that, using the standards taught by our civilisation to be the correct ones, the recipients seem to be the wrong 'uns. Do our problems in society come from our readiness to place our future in the hands of politicians, who rarely are unselfish enough to wield correctly the great power entrusted to them? Have we been spineless in failing to make them be subject to the will of the people and allowing them instead to take the power to be our masters? Why has our nation been deprived of the benign influence of men like Bill, Johnny and Commander Hawkins upon our young generations and allowed it to be supplanted by the evil entertainment of some promiscuous, drug-crazed, empty-minded, hip thrusting, caterwauling performers on guitars? Many of our youngsters want it that way, and seem to resent any advice to the contrary because that would be to accept some sort of debt to the society we live in. Goodness knows that servicemen of my generation and our forefathers have paid ten times over for what we have and consider ourselves to be lucky to come through with our lives. At least I assert my earned right to express my opinions even if they are thought to be worthless and anti-social. Perhaps my subliminal purpose in writing this account is to bring home to the more sensitive members of the young generations the facts dormant behind the notion of "self sacrifice".

Chapter Twenty

The Final Act

It is extremely selfish to look upon the end of the war from a European point of view. The most vicious war at sea was yet to come in the Pacific with the most awful expenditure of men and machines; but our weariness was such that we wanted to rest on our laurels and take a breather, in spite of knowing that perhaps the worst part still lay ahead.

In the last spring of the European War there could be no relaxation. Germany was being forced back on to her home territory. It is natural to defend one's homeland with desperation and that is what happened. Her men at sea picked up world news from whatever source they could, all of it being bad. Air raids on submariners' home cities and news of Russian advances into the German hinterland could and did destroy the morale of these men. Their one wish was to be by the side of their loved ones, to defend them from the retribution due to be inflicted upon them by Russians who had experienced the barbarism of German forces at Stalingrad and Leningrad, or by RAF bomb-aimers, whose families had borne the brunt of Luftwaffe operations over the east end of London. Atlantic U-boat crews knew they must run the gauntlet of Allied ships and aircraft all the way back into the Baltic, now that all the U-boat bases in France had been over-run by Allied troops, so the chance of getting back safely to their families was diminishing day by day. At the same time, Germans were well aware of the fate of their troops who fell into the hands of the Russians and disappeared, without trace and in most cases, for ever. Would it be better to surrender to the western Allies than to be caught later by the Russians? The temptation in the Atlantic was to carry on fighting to the bitter end, hoping for chivalrous treatment, but Hitler's suicide crumpled further resistance.

Just days before the end of the war in Europe, our SOE dropped a pattern of depth charges around a periscope reported in the lane of the convoy ahead of the one which we occupied in the box, and though the periscope had been sighted by three separate ships' lookouts no results were observed. The spot was marked and we flew around it at intervals to see if either debris or a whole submarine might surface, but no luck.

My flying log for the early days of 1945 shows that we tended to patrol ahead further afield than usual, up to eighty nautical miles instead of our usual fifty and with a step-aside of thirty instead of twenty. Here we had a sighting of a U-boat but at such a distant range that we lost sight of it amongst disturbed and breaking seas and had to assume that they saw us and submerged. They had plenty of time to do so, (and also to take in the washing from the jackstay line if they wished) at our closing ground speed of about 40 knots (airspeed of 72 knots with a headwind in the thirties). We dropped a sea marker at the approximate spot and then went away, returning in half an hour hoping that Jerry would think we had gone and that he would resurface. No such luck!

With the Russian ground forces already in the suburbs of Berlin, it was thought that many U-boats might decide to keep on the surface and high-tail for home at maximum speed with the knowledge that the end of the war must be within weeks if not days. However fanatical a U-boat Skipper might be, it could be better to surrender on the surface rather than die below the waves.

On May 6th 1945, I landed back from a dusk patrol to be debriefed, and was met with jubilation because of a message in plain language broadcast by the Admiralty to the effect that offensive action would cease forthwith, provided that the enemy would fly a white flag of surrender and would proceed on the surface to the nearest allied port. Any display of belligerence by the enemy was to be met with immediate retaliation by all means available. After receiving a signal the next day that our aircraft should remain on board to be lifted off by crane in the Clyde, our celebration started in an atmosphere of thankfulness that we had come through so far, but with apprehension concerning what would happen next in the context of the Pacific War. In a spirit of high jinks, we wandered from cabin to cabin throughout the ship. There was no one place big enough to hold all the personnel aboard and everyone wanted to have a drink with everyone else, and to say a thank-you for the help, friendship and rapport which we had shared to our mutual advantage. We all felt indebted to everyone else except to stewards, but even towards them there was tolerance and forgiveness, although it took the end of one war to finish another. Bodies in various states of inebriation littered bunks, settees in saloons, lavatory seats in the heads and floors in companionways. Teetotallers and conscientious personnel, vastly outnumbered by the drunks, took it upon themselves to perform the duties of the irresponsible, to keep us safe as the convoy rounded the South of Ireland and headed up the Irish sea towards the Clyde.

It was at this point that someone at Derby House in Liverpool decided to revoke the instruction that we were to be craned off in the Clyde and, instead, we were to fly to Maydown on May 8th, which was to be celebrated as "Victory in Europe Day" and would be a public holiday, obviously forgetting that everything would close down, including airfields and HM Customs and Excise. I managed to muster enough of my ground crew to check the serviceability of my plane, to rouse Bill and another observer, pack all our belongings for the last time, tie kit and observers safely in the back seats and range my kite for take-off. Feeling very sentimental about my parting from the ship and all my friends, and with a mistiness in my eyes partially induced by alcohol, I said hurried goodbyes and failed to seize the last opportunity to note the addresses of those with whom I wanted to maintain contact. There came the moment to open the throttle and take off, and I was struck with the brilliant idea of giving one last display of superb pilotage to all those who had crawled their way up onto deck and into safety nets, and to line the "goofers" as a token of our brotherhood. Q3 was the one and only serviceable aircraft so it was up to me to give them all a display to keep in their memories.

I climbed to about seven hundred feet so I could dive at full throttle and thus get some speed up, to fly alongside the ship but below deck level so the audience could look down on us while we skimmed the waves. Then a similar run along the other side of the ship so as to give the others the treat which they hadn't been able to see because we had been out of sight below deck level on the opposite side. My next trick was to fly from bow to stern at full throttle, and bounce my wheels along the deck, missing the bridge by a couple of feet, having the painted centre line to guide me accurately. Lastly, in tribute to the Skipper on the bridge I slowed down to nearly stalling and flew alongside the bridge to throw up the smartest Guardsman's salute that I could muster. However my judgement was as clouded by alcohol as was my brain and with my wing, about two feet in from the tip, I carried away one of the ship's aerials. Considerably sobered by realisation of my stupidity, which could have killed dozens besides myself, I climbed up to the cloud base at about one thousand feet, waggling my wings to make sure that I had full control as well as a gesture of farewell. Then I set course, which I had worked out very slowly and quietly before takeoff, for Maydown near Londonderry, knowing full well that the boys in the back seat would have no idea where south was and couldn't care less.

I do not accept a charge of irresponsibility because I had accepted an order not to fly, <u>before</u> taking alcohol in excess. The desire to unwind, after the extremes of stress which we had endured in the previous three years, was hard to suppress at the age of twenty-two. There was concern in our minds about the tasks to which their Lordships of the Admiralty in their ignorance might commit us, and the equipment they would give us to deal with the Japs. Perhaps they would be kind and let us keep our Stringbags in preference to Barracudas?

On reaching the coast of Northern Ireland, I realised that the cloud base was too low for me to fly directly overland to Londonderry, so I stepped aside to fly parallel to the coast keeping well clear of the cliffs and rocky promontories, which are such a lovely feature of that area to the earthbound but not to mariners or aviators. The spectacular Glens of Antrim, Rathlin Island, Dunluce Castle, the Giant's Causeway, the White Rocks, Portrush, Portstewart, Castlerock and Magilligan Point opening the mouth of Lough Foyle, all went past like a travelogue and then we were back to Maydown. As we approached the circuit I was amazed to see more than a dozen U-boats already tied up side by side outside Londonderry, and I flew round a couple of times because my back-seat passengers were recovering from their haze and expressing an interest in the world around them. Not for the want of trying, it was the nearest we had ever been to the craft we had hated, feared and grudgingly admired so much.

Seeing no signs of life on the airfield I flew low over the control tower without raising a soul, so landed and taxied in to a deserted tarmac dispersal and cut my engine. I was not inclined to leave our kit unattended, and I was also conscious of the contraband cigarettes and spirits secreted in the body of the aircraft. Nor was I inclined to walk the mile and a half to the wardroom. With the excuse at the back of my mind "Don't you know the War is over?" I loaded my Very pistol with a two-star red cartridge and fired it vertically, followed by a three-star green, then another two-star red. These pyrotechnics were drawn to the attention of the Master-at-Arms who, in turn, notified the Duty Officer, who had retired to his cabin and was resentful at being disturbed. Thinking that only a Brass Hat would be sanctioned to fly on VE Day the duty bod got into his Utilicon van and ventured out to find out who and what we were. He was suitably disgruntled to find three improperly and scruffily dressed Sub Lieutenants with obvious hangovers, lounging about waiting to give him some work to do. We wasted no time in off-loading our gear into his Utilicon and being delivered to the wardroom. There we found a Petty Officer Wren used to dealing with flights of 836 Squadron who came and went at inconsiderate hours without rhyme or reason, and she fixed us up with a meal, bed and bedding. What was more important, she found the President of the Wardroom and sought permission to open wine bills for us as a pressing emergency in view of our desperate need for a hair of the dog, which had bitten us the previous day.

We collected our mail and hurried off to the Nissen hut allocated to us and lay on our beds to get up to date on news from home; always the most important thing after time at sea. I sorted mine into four piles: Girlfriend, Mother, Family, and Others, then the first two into chronological order. After reading the most recent from Reta and from home, just to make sure I had the latest news, I started on the oldest ones and slowly worked my way through, savouring every little titbit as I went. Full of optimism, I was hoping for some home leave before heading for the Pacific, but knew that there would be sheer chaos in the Squadron Office next day, because there would not be any instructions and no-one would be prepared to make any decisions until the policy of My Lords of the Admiralty was made known, for fear of cutting across Their wishes, and thus blighting prospects of promotion for ever.

As forecast, the following day was a complete shambles, as it must have been in Berlin but without the raping and looting, (as far as we know). We occupied ourselves by spiriting away the bottles and other contraband from their hiding-places in the recesses of the wings of Q3, under holes in the fabric made good with linen and dope. The Maydown ground crew were well versed in the procedure and, of course, shared in the benefits in proportion to the size of the haul of loot. Our consciences were salved by the biblical exhortation "muzzle not the ox that treadeth out the corn". Operation completed and all sewn up, we telephoned the Master-at-Arms at the Regulating Office, and asked him to tell Customs and Excise at Londonderry that we had landed from sea, wished to clear Customs, and had items to declare, though not very much because of shortage of dollars.

Two days later, a two-ringed old-hand Customs Officer, attended by a very new and very young officer, turned up at the wardroom, and asked to see the new arrivals who had signed-in as required. We were notified and while we were making our way to see them they were supplied with the Guinness the Customs had come to expect as a custom. Delay occasioned by our need to find bicycles meant that they were on their third glass of 'the black stuff' by the time we got there. We were greeted by the older man like long lost friends, and by the younger man with the ring of confidence showing he expected rapid promotion for catching a gang of bullion smugglers -us- who had avoided arrest by generations of old and incompetent Revenue Men like his colleague. After discussion about the partition of Germany, with heartfelt comment about the long-standing partition of Ireland, and then descriptions of the U-boats and their crews arriving almost hourly in Lough Foyle and how our friends reacted to drinking Schnapps with them - such vile stuff compared to the velvet of Guinness, and by the way your glass is empty again and you won't mind if you do, and if you want to see what we have to declare it is down the road in our Nissen hut but it doesn't amount to much and we can organise a couple of bikes for you to ride down there or if you are in a hurry we'll give you a crossbar ride instead but it is hardly worth the effort and now it is getting late and the Camp 'bus goes into Londonderry in forty minutes and there is just time for another glass and yes, a visit to the loo - it is just through that door and second on the left - and yes of course we will have them filled up again for good luck and we know that you'll do the same for us when we come to visit you.

They were seen safely on the 'bus, the older man with his uniform cap pillowing his head against the window and soon fast asleep taking up a whole seat, and the younger one with his investigative enthusiasm dampened but his amorous instincts aroused, was trying to hold the hand of a rather plain but well-turned-out Wren and was being egged on by her Wren companions. Unfortunately, because we felt sure that they had many experiences to recount, we heard nothing more from them.

Next day things began to take shape. Bill and Johnny were to be given home leave and I was briefed to prepare myself for the job of collecting Swordfish from Naval Air Stations in Scotland. Although at the time I accepted the need to dispose of many of these surplus aircraft, as they had no operational use against the Japanese, it was only in later life that I realised the sheer vandalism which I was instructed to perpetrate. I would load up to four pilots in the back seats of my Stringbag and fly them to a Naval Air Station such as Machrihanish, Evanton, Abbotsinch, Ayr or Donibristle, collect our Swordfish and fly them to Barton Airfield four miles west of Manchester for scrapping.

At Barton, paraffin was splashed over the Swordfish which was then torched to give the poor old warhorse a Vikings' cremation. The incombustible remains, copper, brass, aluminium, duralumin, steel and cast iron were all compressed into a block about a metre cubed, dropped into a pit and covered with earth. When I had the task of taking the Stringbag, which had served me so well in Q Flight at sea, in for euthanasia it was just like taking a tried and trusting old hound into the vet to be put down. I went prepared with spanners, screwdriver and sheath-knife intending to avail myself of the control column and the canvas of the fuselage bearing the letters M3Q, out of which I could make a table lamp and shade.

Unfortunately I was observed helping myself and I was stopped at the gate by a very young and officious Officer of the Day, an RAF Pilot Officer without pilot's wings, (called a "Penguin" by aircrew) who threatened to charge me with the theft of Government property and I had no choice but to hand over my booty. My reason for wanting what was going to be scrap of no value fell on deaf ears and I had to listen to the insulting comment that an officer of my experience and seniority should have known better but, in view of my service, and the fact that there were no "other ranks" involved, I could surrender the stolen goods and would not be charged with the offence. About a day later, when the head of steam pressure had subsided in my brain and I returned to rational thought, I realised that the third party who had observed and reported my activity could have been anyone from the Station Commander downwards and the poor young Pilot Officer had no choice but to stop me. But it did seem a shame.

After clearing Maydown's surplus Swordfish it was decided that it would be more efficient for my action base to be Donibristle on the Firth of Forth and, accordingly, I was drafted there. On the day following my transfer, Reta, who had joined the WRNS, completed her initial training, qualified as a Coder and promoted to Leading Wren, arrived at Maydown, to find me gone. For a considerable length of time I had to protest that my move was neither avoidance nor evasion, especially because Reta made enquiries of me from a very plain and unattractive stewardess, who worked in the wardroom, and was told by her how nice I was, that she had a crush on me, and that I had given her a Canadian chocolate bar which wasn't very nice but it was a lovely token. Get out of that one, Stanley. It took several closely written sheets of paper before normal communications were restored.

Reta used to tell the story of her experiences at Maydown, where the signals office was situated on the side of the airfield opposite to the site of the Wrennery and, although it was "manned" by Wrens around the clock every day of the week, it had outside chemical toilets and was without running water. The signals officer used to make unscheduled visits at any time of day or night, and always demanded a fresh brew of tea from the Wrens, making in-roads on their ration of tea and depleting the supply of water which the girls had to bring in bottles and jars from the Wrennery as they came on duty. One morning, Wrens from two different shifts were off-duty and taking coffee in the canteen and the subject of the signal officer's tea demands came up in conversation. The afternoon shift told how they ran out of carried water, so they had made him tea from water in the fire-bucket, whereupon the night shift collapsed in hysterical giggling. When this subsided enough for them to become coherent, they confessed that because of the cold, the dark, and those horrible chemical toilets, more than one of the girls had used the fire bucket to relieve calls of nature.

Remote from all this, I wended my way around the U.K, collecting Swordfish as I went. On one occasion, with two others in formation with me, I ran into thick fog coming down the

Northumberland coast, and had to find somewhere to put down until it cleared. I was not familiar enough with Tyneside to head inland to the aerodrome there, so continued down the coast at about one hundred and fifty feet above the sea, knowing the cliffs at Marsden, just north of Sunderland, were the highest obstacles en route, until reaching the mouth of the River Tees where I was on familiar territory. My boyhood home was at South Bank, which as implied by the name, was on the south bank of the Tees and I knew every street and slagheap in the district. At five o'clock in the evening, just as the locals finished work for the day, my formation of three good old bumbling Swordfish appeared through the fog, and skirted the clock tower of St. Peter's church. We were seen by nearly everyone who worked at Dorman Long Steelworks at Dormanstown, the coke ovens and blast furnaces at Grangetown, Smiths Dock at South Bank, Cargo Fleet Iron and Steel, and then by all the commercial and shop workers of Middlesbrough setting off for home. I followed the roads which I had cycled on my way to Thornaby Aerodrome as a boy and dismissed my wingmen one at a time over the hedge at the beginning of the runway, and followed them round to see them safely down. It was the hedge where I had lain all those years ago watching the Wapitis, Hawker Harts, Hawker Hinds and, on rare occasions, even a Gloster Gladiator, which had made me long to fly. At the control tower we reported to the RAF Duty Officer who was flabbergasted by our unannounced arrival, saying that all flying was suspended from Berwick to the Channel Islands and all aerodromes closed. I took the opportunity to misquote Bill Thomson saying, "Only birds and fools fly, but only the Fleet Air Arm gets through on a day like this".

Before my Swordfish vandalism was completed, I had to hand the task over to others and report to Lee-on-the-Solent for a quick conversion course as a night-fighter pilot in Fairey Fireflies, which were two-seater monoplanes, very similar in appearance to the Spitfire to a casual observer. It had everything one might expect in a modern combat machine and was a delight to fly, with comfort included. I was given twelve hours of solo flight to familiarise myself with the aircraft before joining No.1 Operational Training

Unit at Inskip once more, where I had to go through the procedure of crewing-up again. I will never understand why the powers-that-be could not apply the simple expedient of reuniting Bill Thomson with me instead of going through all the hassle of trying to recreate the amalgam of personalities so essential in a crew. Under the surface I resented the split-up of our partnership and knew that it could never be replaced, which doomed any relationship with another Observer right from the start. I suspect that my reaction was as it would have been if ever I had experienced a second marriage, and I found myself forever drawing unwarranted comparisons between the two.

There was some joy to be obtained in the next fifty hours of operational training because of the sheer exhilaration obtained from opening the throttle of the responsive Rolls Royce Griffon engine and cavorting in a variety of breathtaking manoeuvres around clumps of cotton-wool cumulus cloud. However, there was a vivid sense of urgency to defeat the Japanese forces which so far had given the impression of being invincible, so the navigational exercises, bombing, machine-gun firing, and the devastating fire-power of our twin cannon had to be practised to near perfection. My determination was enhanced by the news that my cousin Frank had been killed in his Seafire in the Pacific, causing heartbreak to his poor parents.

We did not know it at that time, of course, but the end of the war with the Japanese was only weeks away. It was ended by America's difficult decision to drop two atomic bombs on the Japanese homeland, at Hiroshima and Nagasaki. Whatever the moral rights and wrongs were and though it cost so many lives of women, children and other non-combatants, it prevented the war continuing, perhaps for years, in bitter hand-to-hand attrition with fanatical devotees of the Emperor, and causing the deaths of countless Allied servicemen. That decision possibly saved my life too.

Demobilisation followed amazingly rapidly. An emotional revulsion against any form of authoritarianism fermented throughout the Forces, and an intellectual resentment sprang up against any activity designed to "keep the men busy". It became of paramount importance to disperse potential mutineers and revolutionaries who would not accept occupations such as whitewashing coal in the fuel-buckets. Such people, provided with one of the Fifty Shilling Tailors' suits, a trilby hat, shoes, socks and a raincoat were sent out to re-establish themselves with a War Gratuity which could be drunk away in one night by those so inclined. No one was surprised when they voted out Winston Churchill and elected a Labour Government.

What a disaster the Brave New World has been!

I was lucky in that, under the Further Education and Training Scheme for ex-servicemen, I was allowed to recommence my education at the point where it had been interrupted. I was not allowed to change course to study medicine as I wished, which proved to be a good thing. My later experience in industry taught me that I was unfitted to judge the point at which I had done everything, which I could reasonably be expected to do. I could never leave my work until it was as complete as I was able to make it. In industry this attitude led to ridiculously long hours of work and I now realise that, in medicine, I would have become so emotionally involved with dying patients that I would have found it impossible to leave them in case I could find some way of helping them. I would never have made a good doctor and would have killed myself by trying unreasonably hard.

After acquiring a BSc (Hons.) Chem. Dunelmensis, I did shiftwork as Plant Superintendent at Manchester Oil Refinery more as a Chemical Engineer than Chemist. I then joined an engineering company, which manufactured machinery for the dairy, brewing and soft drinks industries. But that is another story!

Chapter Twentyone

What Did Macships Achieve?

If we are to judge by the awareness of the general public, official publicity or the number of decorations awarded to personnel who served in Macships, then Macships might never have existed. In the course of the last fifteen years I have been contacted by several researchers gathering information on which to base documentaries for television and radio and with two exceptions one of their early questions was "How many submarines did you sink".

When my answer was "None" all interest seemed to disappear and a researcher blinkered to this degree is unworthy of the name. I was not given the opportunity to explain that a submarine forced to dive or kept underwater was made impotent, unless it was already in a position of its own choice, of strategic importance relative to a prospective victim. To submerge, a submarine had to shut down its diesel engine, which would have given it a speed of seventeen knots on the surface and instead, use its battery-driven electric motors which gave an underwater top speed of six knots for a very limited period, after which it would be forced to surface to recharge the batteries. In the absence of air cover, the U-boat would race ahead of the convoy, on the surface at seventeen knots and recharge its batteries as it went, using its diesel engines. Free to select its optimum position to attack, it would then submerge and wait for the victims to approach making small and quiet movements as necessary by electrical power. After attacking it would lie quietly below until the convoy had moved on, then it would surface, switch over to diesel propulsion and race at full speed around the flank of the convoy, out of range of the escorts' detection devices, to take up position once again ahead of the convoy to create mayhem once more. So it would go on, night after night, exhausting all the defences and sinking ships faster than they could be replaced. The presence of air cover immediately altered all this by depriving the enemy of the speedy transit on the surface and if, by luck, a U-boat happened to be in a fortuitously advantageous position to press home an attack, it was impossible for it to have a second go without incurring unacceptable risk.

In the nine months before Escort Carriers and Macships were introduced, the total number of merchant ships sunk in the Atlantic was three hundred and sixty-two, whereas in the nine months afterwards the number dropped to sixty-one. In convoys escorted by Macships, from their first voyage in April 1943 to the end of the European War in May 1945 only two merchant ships were sunk. These two U-boat successes were achieved only by the use of acoustic torpedoes, which homed onto the propeller noise of a victim and did not require the attacker to take up a precise position, and gave success by accident rather than design.

In mid-1942, when Doenitz had 320 operational U-boats, they sank 624,000 tons of our merchant ships in one month. At the end of the war in Europe 376 U-boats either surrendered or scuttled themselves. Many were of better design and performance than their predecessors, backed up by 'milch cow' supplies, allowing U-boats to spend more time on patrol and less in transit to base. Their crews were experienced and seasoned, yet they achieved so little success against convoys protected by Macships, because the very threat from our Swordfish kept them under.

The Battle of the Atlantic was not won by Macships, but if they had been introduced in early 1940 they might well have done so, and many Merchant Navy seamen who were sacrificed would be alive today. I will not use the euphemism 'they gave their lives' because they didn't voluntarily give, except in a very few cases which should have been recognised by the award of a posthumous V.C. Their lives were taken from them, often due to the crass stupidity of people who should have known better.

Macships were not magic wands to ensure victory because German bravery, dedication and devotion to their cause would have encouraged U-boat crews to develop the anti-aircraft U-boat equipped with multiple cannon to stay on the surface and fight it out with our aircraft. Later the development of the snorkel, a venting device for diesel exhaust gases whilst running submerged at full speed, would largely counter our advantage of having an aircraft near a convoy to force a U-boat into impotent and slow submerged passage.

Who knows how many ships survived because a U boat saw a Swordfish whose crew, because of poor visibility, bad light, rough seas or exposure to cold didn't even see the U-boat? Our presence alone was a deterrent, which could make U-boats submerge, where their offensive potential was minimised. I'm glad my colleagues and I were there and we would not have wished it any other way. We had pride in what we did and what we achieved, however little that might appear to be to those who were not there.

----ooOoo----

The Fairey Firefly Mk.1

Epilogue

As We Who Are Left Grow Old

It is the 8th of May in the year 2001. This is the anniversary of Victory in Europe Day (VE Day) 1945 and it is also the 60th birthday of Swordfish W5856 which survived my attempt to write her off at Errol in early 1944. (See Chapter 11). A small group of distinguished-looking people have been brought together at the Queen's Hotel, Leeds, by Barry V. Brand, the General Manager of the Leeds branch of the supporters of the Swordfish Historic Flight, who have persuaded Leeds City Council to adopt the resurrected W5856 which has been flying again since it was totally rebuilt in 1994. The group are dining together in the Queen's Hotel at Leeds, all of them around their fourscore years and bonded together by their lifelong affection for the Swordfish. These men, nearly all decorated for gallantry in the face of the enemy, went into battle in one of these so-called obsolete open-cockpit biplanes, which commanded loyalties similar to those that the knights of old had for their steeds. Swordfish were loyal war-horses, which could be trusted and relied upon never to falter in the face of exposure to the elements and opposition from the enemy, even when prevented by the harshness of the environment from receiving the richly deserved attention to their needs. They saw action in the Channel Dash of the Scharnhorst and Gneisenau, the destruction of the Italian Fleet at Taranto, the sinking of four ships with three torpedoes in Bomba Harbour, the crippling of the Bismark, created the principle of "pathfinders", enabling Wellingtons to effectively bomb German concentrations in the Western Desert, and faced the grey horrors of the U-boat war in the Battle of the Atlantic and in the Russian Convoys.

Why meet at Leeds? Because in the grim early days of the 1939-1945 war, Leeds adopted the aircraft carrier HMS Ark Royal, and gave generously of their moral and financial support to the crew and the nation. Then, when the Ark was sunk in the Mediterranean in 1941, Leeds held a "Warships Week" in which they raised over £9,300,000 in the currency of the day, which was worth many tens of that in today's value of the pound. Their unstinting support for the Fleet Air Arm has continued unabated to the present day, and the tradition is now so firmly established that we can be sure that it will continue through the good offices of future Mayors and Corporations.

In such distinguished company, I felt very humble, undecorated and without a kill to my name. Macships had no sweeping victories or banner headlines. There was far more fear than heroism in our work, but overcoming sustained hazards round the clock for months on end without leave or other respite can be even more dependent upon guts, than making an instantaneous decision to tackle a remorseless enemy when backed up by a rush of adrenaline. I am convinced that, but for our presence, our merchant shipping would have suffered far more casualties than it did. So, at the same time, I knew that my participation in this gathering was justified, to represent the efforts of all those who served in the Macships 836 and 860 Squadron Wing, not one of whom received any recognition whatsoever of their contribution to the defeat of the U-boat, not even the nineteen Merchant Navy Skippers who, after a two-week course found themselves Captain of an Aircraft Carrier looking after a convoy of up to 150 ships going through 'U-boat Alley'.

It was quite late as we left. The fitful lights of the street lamps gave the impression that they were swinging a little. The deck was rising and falling through a good few feet as the cool night air took hold. There was more than a degree or two of roll as well, giving a long-forgotten figure-of-eight motion to our bows. Instinctively, we reached out to our Stringbag 'oppos', and immediately we found that mutual support which could be expected as of right, and so freely given in the past. Where else could you be so sure of such immediate response? We were airborne, well tanked up, in the best company in the world, facing adverse conditions with the utmost confidence, and our morale was so high that it was decorum alone, which prevented us from bursting into song. We knew also that, as always, we had the backup of our ground crew and other supporters waiting to sort out our unserviceabilities if we called for their help. They never had, and never would, let us down.

Were those days really so long ago? Yes, a very long time ago, in fact, a lifetime ago. Age <u>has</u> wearied us, and the years <u>have</u> condemned. Even so, Stringbags are still flying, and with so much goodwill towards them, they will continue to do so long after the last of us has been written off the manifest. Perhaps the last Stringbag will waggle her wings in salute to the thousands of aircrew who shared the fate of her predecessors and bequeathed a proud heritage and example to generations of men and machines to come.

Two Songs From A Macship Saloon

Words by Sub Lieutenant (A) Jack Thomas RNVR 836 Squadron

To the tune of the "Ovaltinies"

We are the Macship "heroes"
Famous for our "do"es
A bunch of worn-out Naviators
Badly need rejuvenators.
Would you like a U-boat story,
Tales to thrill you all?
A thousand lines we shoot when frisky,
But all we sink is gin and whisky,
We never fly – it's far too risky,
Merry Macship boys.

To the tune of "Don't fence me in"

Oh give me wings, lots of wings with no canopy above,
Don't fence me in.
Take me back to the wide open "Stringbag" that I love,
Don't fence me in.
Let me watch the valves a-popping as each cylinder fires,
Listen to the music of those bracing wires,
Keep your Barracudas and your new Seafires,
Don't fence me in.

One-plank aeroplanes are not for me.
If I really have to fly then let it be
Two-plank aeroplanes - or better still three
Don't fence me in

Requiem For Bill And Johnny

Bill Thomson was killed a few years after the war, when as a married man with two children he was with a club climbing in Glencoe. The club was alerted to the fact that a Sheffield University student was in difficulties on a rock face and could go neither up, down, nor sideways. By the time Bill and his club mates arrived at the spot, the student was in a state of panic but Bill volunteered to go to his help even though it was a difficult spot with an overhang, which prevented rope support from above. Bill reached the student, who in panic clutched at Bill and struggled, causing Bill to lose his hold and they both fell to their deaths. How does one pay tribute to a man like Bill, who was brave but not fearless? I, alone, was aware of his fears only because I saw him in disturbed sleep (in our shared cabin) after the rebuilt aircraft and wing locking-pin incidents. How many more incidents were there in his lifetime, other than the three of which I know, where Bill would risk everything he valued when he knew that someone else's life was in danger but he could see that it was within his power to help? He was a gentleman and a friend indeed, and a natural hero in addition.

After demobilisation Johnny Hopkins found it impossible to settle into civilian routine and he was worried about his prospects in the printing company he worked for, because he was too old for an apprenticeship but too young to earn an adult wage. Knowing that he was unable to support his widowed mother, who was in poor health and unable to support herself, he tried to kill her and himself. This was the only time I know of where Johnny did a botched job. Police took him to Horton Mental Hospital for Certification and treatment. After several months of institutional life during which Johnny used his unarmed combat training in attempts to escape, a pre-frontal leucotomy was carried out on him, severing the front lobes of his brain and resulting in him losing all initiative and interest in life. In effect, he was reduced to the state of a cabbage, and he failed to recognise either Bill or myself in our separate visits even though we had been closer than brothers. I had failed him in his time of need, having been responsible for that need. War, and its aftermath, is Hell and let no-one forget it. I never will.

War, however, made boys into Men, if it didn't break them. It also taught that with shared experience of being "blooded", and the faith in each other that such experience can bring, men can become as close as brothers without the conventional blood relationship.